MR. WILL[IAM]
# SHAKESP[EARE]
## COMEDIES
## HISTORIE[S]
## TRAGEDI[ES]

Published according to the True [Originals]

Martin Droeshout sculpsit London.

LONDO[N]
Printed by Isaac Iaggard, and Ed[ward]

**PORTRAITS OF GREATNESS**

General Editor
ENZO ORLANDI

Text by
MARIA PIA ROSIGNOLI
Translator
MARY KANANI

Published 1968 by
The Hamlyn Publishing Group Ltd
Hamlyn House, The Centre,
Feltham, Middlesex
© 1967 Arnoldo Mondadori Editore
Translation © 1968 by
The Hamlyn Publishing Group Ltd
Printed in Italy by
Arnoldo Mondadori, Verona

RES

&

all Copies.

nt. 1623.

# THE LIFE AND TIMES OF
# SHAKESPEARE

**PAUL HAMLYN**
London · New York · Sydney · Toronto

# HONOURED GENTLEMAN OR UPSTART CROW?

England is a mine of documents. Its archives, both municipal and ecclesiastical, overflow with evidence of the past. It is, therefore, all the more suprising that we should know so little of William Shakespeare. The most thorough investigations have revealed only a parish register, a few deeds for the acquisition of houses and land, a summons for disturbing the peace, some evidence of litigation over financial matters, a three-page will in which the signatures, though undoubtedly those of the author, bear little resemblance to each other, and a few of his works published in London under his own name during his lifetime (though these were but a small proportion of the total number of his works), and that is all. However, we do also possess the references made to him by his contemporaries—far more alive than the dry, legal jargon —which throw light on the personality of the great dramatist. The first reference to him is an uncomplimentary one: Robert Greene, a poet, roused to an insane jealousy, described him as "a tyger's heart wrapt in a player's hide", and "an upstart crow beautified with our feathers". This is virtually the only discordant note in a chorus of praise and admiration. After the death of Greene the publisher who had printed the attack publicly begged Shakespeare's pardon, assuring him that he personally believed him to be "no less civil than he excellent in the quality he professes; besides, divers of worship have reported his uprightness of dealing which argues his honesty". Ben Jonson, doyen of Elizabethan writers, said of Shakespeare after his death: "I loved the man and do honour his memory on this side idolatry as much as any. He was, indeed, honest and of an open, free nature." In an Elizabethan text the words honesty and honest mean far more than they do today, their modern equivalent being nearer to honour and honourable. If we add to these and other testimonials a background of Elizabethan England and, above all, such information as can be gathered from Shakespeare's works themselves, we can begin to reconstruct a picture of this extraordinary actor and gentleman, whose life straddled two centuries and two reigns and who, in the space of 20 years, wrote 154 sonnets, several poems and 37 comedies and tragedies, many of which are acknowledged masterpieces.

The county of Warwickshire, lying in the heart of England, north-west of London, is known for its pleasant, undulating countryside. On the left is Aston Cantlow, not far from Stratford-on-Avon, where Shakespeare's parents lived. Above: the ancient house of Wilmcote—a village also near Stratford—bearing the notice "Mary Arden's House". Mary Arden was Shakespeare's mother. The houses of the period were built of wood and stone or brick, with thatched roofs. The lower picture shows a countrywoman going by horse to market with her wares. It is a print from the Album Amicorum compiled by George Holzschuer in the early sixteenth century.

5

# HIS FATHER AN IMPORTANT CITIZEN, HIS MOTHER A GENTLEWOMAN

Stratford-on-Avon is a market town in the county of Warwickshire on the River Avon about a hundred miles from London. William Shakespeare was born towards the end of April in the year 1564 in a comfortable black-beamed house in Henley Street, where his family had moved a year or so previously. With the beginning of spring the river was swollen from the thaw, and the fields were golden with daffodils. A few days after his birth, on April 26, the child was baptized in the parish church of the Holy Trinity. The parish register bears the inscription "1564—April 26, Gulielmus filius Johannes Shakespeare". Stratford was then a town of about 1,500 inhabitants. A contemporary historian describes it as *emporium non inelegans,* a town not without charm. Its houses were overlooked by the church and by the stone tower of the town hall. The surrounding countryside was green and undulating and the woods were full of game. In winter people gathered around the fireside to listen to tales of long ago. In summer the youth of the town met in the nearby Forest of Arden, and strange tales were told of its witches and hobgoblins. The young William grew up in those lively rural surroundings inhabited by well-to-do farmers, wealthy merchants, travellers eager to tell of the happenings in London, and arrogant yet generous noblemen. Stratford was a small town and everyone there knew everything about everyone else. One day a young girl named Charlotte Hamlett was found drowned in the green waters of the Avon. The verdict of the inquest was suicide for reasons of love and she was denied burial in consecrated ground. Her parents maintained that it was a case of accidental death, that the young girl had slipped while trying to pick marsh flowers. The case was discussed for a long time. The documents relating to the inquest are still in the archives at Stratford. The young Shakespeare listened and remembered. We can imagine him as a boy with an oval face, regular features, large dark eyes and a small mouth. His family was respected in Stratford. His father, John, held a number of important posts from the curious one of ale-taster to that of bailiff. His mother, Mary Arden, was the daughter of a neighbouring landowner whose family bore its own coat-of-arms, and she was considered to be a gentlewoman.

# MERRY ENGLAND

The origins of John Shakespeare, William's father, were humble. His parents worked on the land for Sir Robert Arden at Wilmcote, a small village not far from Stratford. The Ardens were among the better families of Warwickshire, dating back to the Norman Conquest. Ambitious and clever, John was not content to remain a small tenant farmer. He set himself up as a glove-maker, and when he acquired sufficient means he asked his master for the hand of his daughter, Mary Arden, in marriage. The wedding took place in 1557, and Mary became a faithful and devoted wife. There were eight children of whom William was the third. John Shakespeare had now gained a foothold in the local aristocracy and his own fortune had been substantially increased by the two small farms which were his wife's dowry. He was therefore able to build up and expand his business. Documents describe him as a merchant in wool, grain and meat. It is likely that he owned a shop from which he was able to sell the produce of his land. He was considered honest and shrewd and he took great interest in the public life of Stratford. He was appointed Justice of the Peace, Assessor of Fines, Alderman and, in 1569, Bailiff. He was then at the peak of his wealth which was to decline steadily, whether from his generosity to the town or his fondness for lawsuits is not known. Part of his duty as bailiff was officially to receive travelling actors on behalf of the Earl of Worcester, and in 1569 a company of actors arrived in Stratford. William was only five years old, but it is likely that he joined in the festivities. John Shakespeare spent a sizeable part of the municipal funds in royally entertaining the players, as was the custom of the day. Public festivities were very much in fashion in an England that was merry and refined, and somewhat boisterous as well. The fairs and market-places were full of jugglers, acrobats and wandering minstrels. On the hills of the Cotswolds, not far from Stratford, wrestling and archery contests were held and sports of every kind took place. Shakespeare must have known all these things at first-hand and he describes them in *As You Like It* and other plays.

On the opposite page two scenes are shown from the time of Shakespeare: above, a water-carrier; below, a wedding banquet. Even in the smaller towns the costumes were rich. Note the musicians and monkey near the balustrade. On this page is a view of the church of the Holy Trinity, Stratford, surrounded by ancient elm trees. It was here that William Shakespeare was baptized and it is here that he lies buried. The bottom left picture shows a page from the parish register which clearly records Shakespeare's christening. On the right is the page relating to his death. As it was the custom to baptize infants within two or three days of their birth, it is presumed that the poet was born on April 23, the day of St. George, Patron Saint of England. His sign of the zodiac was therefore Taurus. Those born under this sign, it is said, are attached to the land, very ambitious, constantly trying to improve themselves and capable of intensive work—all traits which may be seen in Shakespeare's character.

ACTVS IIII. SCENA II.

ACTVS III. SCENA IIII.

ACTVS IIII. SCENA

# LATIN AND GREEK FOR THE YOUNG WILLIAM

*Ben Jonson, Shakespeare's friend and rival, said of him that he knew "small Latin and less Greek". What he did know he had learned at school. On the opposite page are three scenes from the comedies of Terence which were used in the schools as Latin texts. Below them is a picture of the main hall at Stratford Grammar School.*

*Below, a picture of Harvard House, Stratford, an example of the middle-class dwelling of Shakespeare's time; also the frontispieces of three books very much in use at the time: The Book of Common Prayers (1552), The Schoolmaster by Roger Ascham, Queen Elizabeth's tutor, and the 1568 translation of the Holy Bible.*

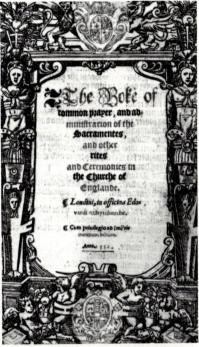

"And then the whining schoolboy, with his satchel and shining morning face, creeping like snail unwillingly to school." This description from *As You Like It* could easily be an echo of Shakespeare's own childhood, as could the scene in *The Merry Wives of Windsor* where a Welsh priest submits a boy (who incidentally is named William) to a stupid Latin examination. Shakespeare's father may have been illiterate; he on the other hand was sent to school, and so in all probability were his three surviving brothers and his sister. This would indicate not only his father's social status but also the great changes that had begun to take place in England during that time. The country had just ended a long period of war. There had been the Hundred Years' War, the War of the Roses and much fighting under Henry VIII and his children Edward VI and Mary Tudor. These upheavals had prevented England from participating in the great intellectual awakening that had transformed Europe. The great literary scholars of France and Italy considered the English little more than barbarians and were not greatly interested in her as a neighbour. Elizabeth's accession to the throne in 1558 brought peace to the country, at least on home ground, and England was now able to make up for lost time. The spirit of the age awoke a richness of talent which formed the core of the English Renaissance. Schooling was now as much for the sons of tradesmen and farmers as for the sons of gentlemen. The translation and wide circulation of the Bible, with its own religious wars, had given many people a taste for reading and for poetic language. At school, boys learned the Latin and Greek classics, studying the works of Seneca, Plato, Terence and Ovid. Booksellers stocked the latest Italian novels and French poems translated into English, and various chronicles of the history of England. It was one of the accomplishments of a gentleman to write a sonnet and many of the populace understood the mythological references with which the writing of the time is crammed. Some such knowledge, half-digested, lay behind the remark of the Hostess in *Henry V* who, mourning the death of Falstaff, gives assurance that "He's in Arthur's bosom", replacing the biblical Abraham with King Arthur, who was a more homely figure, and closer to England.

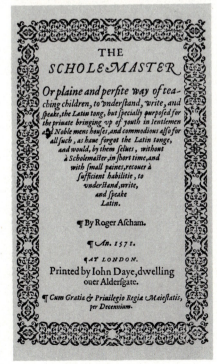

# FAMILY MISFORTUNE AND INTERRUPTED STUDIES

*The picture below shows the trial of Mary Queen of Scots, from a print of the period. She maintained that she was the rightful heir to the English throne through her descent from Henry VII and declared Elizabeth to be an "illegitimate bastard". Mary fought Elizabeth all her life until in 1568 Elizabeth was obliged to imprison her. She was to remain in prison for nearly 20 years during which time she never ceased her conspiracies. The final plot to be uncovered was the cause of her downfall. Her trial was attended by 43 noblemen; she conducted her own defence resolutely but was found guilty and condemned to death. Her execution took place on February 8, 1587.*

We do not know whether the young William, who was sent to Stratford Grammar School at the age of seven, was a good scholar. It seems likely that he was, however, considering his innate curiosity and extraordinary capacity for understanding the most varied subjects, which are borne out by inspection of his later works. We do know that his studies were cut short owing to his father's financial difficulties. From 1576 onwards John Shakespeare ran into debt. He was obliged to raise a mortgage on one of his wife's farms and to sell the other. One of the explanations which have been advanced, and which is supported by the fact that he withdrew gradually from public life, omitting to appear at council meetings until finally his official duties were taken from him, is that both he and his wife may have been Catholics and intended to remain so. England during this time was predominantly Protestant and the Catholics were losing more and more ground. Since Henry VIII's tempestuous separation from the Church of Rome there had been religious persecutions—those of Edward VI against the Catholics and of Mary Tudor against the Protestants. Elizabeth had declared herself to be neither on one side nor the other, avoiding the problem with her customary prudence. The laws pertaining to religious worship had been considerably relaxed, and where once to attend mass might have incurred the death-penalty, it was now possible to practise the Catholic faith so long as it was done discreetly, and in private chapels. Nevertheless Elizabeth's Protestant subjects were less tolerant than she herself was, and they viewed the hated "papists" as Roman spies and enemies of England. National pride went hand in hand with the Protestant religion. Elizabeth's tolerance towards the Catholics came to an abrupt end in 1570 when Pope Pius V excommunicated her and thereby forced her to take sides. Religious conflict began once more, and Mary Stuart, Queen of Scots and claimant to the English throne, was used by the Catholics in their cause, though her frivolous ways did not present a good example of Catholicism to the English people and in fact were seen mainly in contrast to Elizabeth's virtue. Elizabeth was known as the Virgin Queen, the bride of her people, to whom she gave both pride and prosperity.

"The devil is not so much hated as the Pope," wrote the scholar Gabriel Harvey. The English saw in the "papists" above all a political menace, and religious persecution flared up from time to time. The top left picture is a scene from the Martyrology (1583) by John Foxe, showing the execution of the Catholics Latimer and Ridley. The two pictures below are satires on the book A Christall Glass of Christian Reformation, the first one illustrating lust, the second an ironic representation of the doctrine of the salvation of souls in Purgatory. The portrait on the right is of Mary Stuart, by Clouet. Towards the end of her life she wore a wig to hide her white hair.

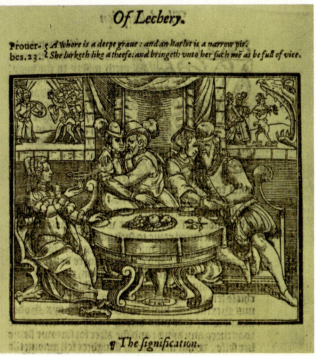

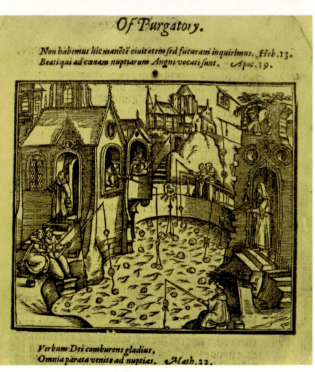

# THE QUEEN'S SPECTACULAR JOURNEYS

*On the opposite page are two pictures of Kenilworth Castle showing it as it is today, above, and as it was in 1620. The taste for country life had spread among the aristocracy towards the end of the sixteenth century and many castles were transformed into stately homes; palaces were being built in less warlike styles and surrounded by nothing more threatening than Italian gardens. Hunting was a popular pastime and the woods that covered England were full of game of every kind. Below are two hunting scenes of* The Noble Art of Venerie and Hunting *and a drawing from a book on falconry. The drawing shows a hunter offering his catch in homage to Elizabeth.*

True to the belief that to be loved a sovereign must be known to her subjects, and be seen by them as much as possible, Elizabeth would frequently travel to her various castles to be near one or other of her courtiers. She made these journeys with a large following and the royal processions, known as "progresses", were a spectacle that attracted great crowds. The Queen knew that pomp and ceremony formed a part of her legend and she took great pains to seem as dazzling as a goddess. On their side, the nobles who entertained her vied with each other in their munificence to satisfy her insatiable appetite for theatrical performances and festivities of every kind. Castles and mansions scattered over the English countryside, which during the wars of the Roses had known scenes of great ferocity, become charming little courts, and their surrounding woods rang with the gay sounds of the royal hunt. Continuous entertainment delighted the guests— music, balls (Elizabeth loved dancing) and plays. In the summer of 1557, when Shakespeare was eleven years old, the Queen and her court took up residence at Kenilworth Castle, thirty miles from Stratford on the opposite bank of the River Avon. Kenilworth, a majestic collection of towers and battlements, was the country residence of Robert Dudley, Earl of Leicester, her childhood companion and favourite on whom she had bestowed the title of Master of the Horse shortly after her accession to the throne. Her stay at Kenilworth was a particularly festive and extravagant one and caused much talk among the loyal subjects of Warwickshire, many of whom were required to help with the outdoor entertainments. Crowds of sightseers must have come from Stratford and members of the council must certainly have visited Kenilworth. One may suppose that the young William accompanied his father at least on one occasion to witness what must have seemed a double attraction—the Queen surrounded by her court as well as the players' performance. This would have been for Shakespeare his second encounter with the theatre, his first being in 1569, but on this occasion it must have made a far stronger impression, presented as it was to his adolescent imagination against the background of Kenilworth Castle and all the luxury of the court, made even more splendid by the Queen's presence.

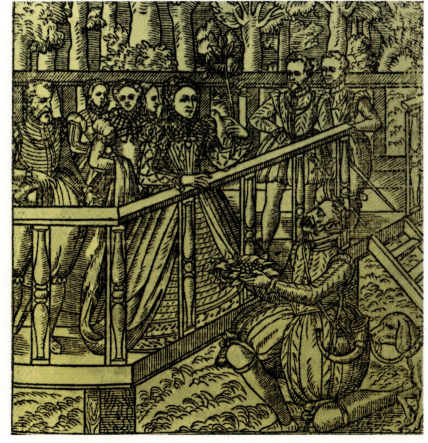

# MARRIAGE AT THE AGE OF EIGHTEEN AND A CHILD ON THE WAY

*The picture below shows the cottage where Shakespeare's wife Ann Hathaway lived before her marriage to the poet. On the right, above, is an autumn scene of the countryside around Stratford with the spire of the Holy Trinity Church reflected in the River Avon. The lower picture, painted by J. Hoefnagel in 1569, shows a country wedding, with open-air dancing and feasting. Although the marriage of Shakespeare to Anne Hathaway had to be arranged rather hastily, they appeared to be very happy, at least in the beginning. The poet's early works express a serene vision of love and a positive image of womanhood.*

Nothing is known of Shakespeare's late boyhood, but if we consider the life of a small country town of that period it is likely that the boy worked first in the corn shop and glove workshop which were his father's main businesses and that later, in order to widen his experience, his father may have asked a friend to take his son as an apprentice. What is certain is that Shakespeare's works accurately describe the ways of life and manner of speech of people in many different trades, suggesting that he had been in close contact with them. There is, for example, a curious reference to the work of the tanner: in a scene from *Hamlet* the grave-digger states that a tanner lasts longer underground than an ordinary mortal, since his skin is so hardened by his trade that it becomes virtually water-proof. His plays are full of images taken from household pursuits—cooking, sweeping, cleaning—from the orchard and the garden, from such sports as bowling, archery and the chase—all of which would have been familiar to an observant boy living in the countryside of Elizabethan England. Our small store of documentary evidence takes us next to the diocesan register of Worcester, which records, in November 1582, the issue of a marriage licence to William Shakespeare and Anne Hathaway. Shakespeare was then 18 years of age and his wife 26—a ripe age for a woman in those days. She was the daughter of a well-to-do local farmer, an old friend of William's father, but brought with her only a small dowry of ten marks (£6 13s 4d). The young William had not made a prosperous marriage and it had been a hasty one. Only six months after the wedding ceremony, in May 1583, a daughter, Susanna, was born. She was always to be his favourite child. Though the marriage had been hurriedly arranged there is nothing to say that the young husband was not very much in love with his wife. In January 1585 twins were born, Judith and Hamnet, named after their godparents, Hamnet and Judith Sadler, who were close friends of the family. Anne Hathaway came from the neighbouring village of Shottery, and after her marriage she came to live at her husband's home in Henley Street where Edmund, Richard, Gilbert and Joan, Shakespeare's brothers and sister, also lived. For a time Shakespeare may have supported his family by working as a teacher.

# THE "NEST OF SWANS" IN THE OPEN SEA

England in those years was a country in ferment. The middle classes were gaining some of the power which hitherto had been in the hands of the aristocracy, many of whom had been killed in the civil wars. Merchants, builders and navigators were at the nerve centre of the age, providing the pillars on which Elizabeth's power rested. New and great opportunities were being offered to Europe from across the Atlantic, and England too reached out to a continent which until then only Spain had touched; vast areas of unexplored lands and riches were there for the taking. On April 27, 1584, the first English expedition set sail financed by Sir Walter Raleigh, the Queen's favourite. The two ships reached land across the ocean nearly three months later. Raleigh, with the gesture of a devoted courtier, dedicated this land to the "Virgin Queen". It was later to become Virginia. At the time of the expedition Shakespeare was twenty years old, married and a father, and apparently destined to become a provincial worthy like his own father. The news from London that swept the country stirred the young especially, and the nephew of a neighbour in Henley Street, a certain Harvard, also left for the American colonies. He was later to make his fortune and to bequeath his wealth to found the university which bears his name to this day. Up to this point relations between Spain and England had been good. The treaty of 1572 had opened the ports of Flanders to English ships and the shipping industry was growing almost daily in size. Elizabeth understood that England's future lay with the sea. And yet this country, which Shakespeare later described with tenderness and admiration as a "Nest of swans in a great pool", was considered barbaric by the rest of Europe. The religious quarrels with Rome and the fact that no one could speak the language, contributed to the opinion that England was nothing but a cold and hostile land.

England was a late starter in the race for the new continent but her enthusiasm compensated for time lost. Expedition followed expedition. In Cymbeline Shakespeare speaks of riding "on the posting winds and doth belie all corners of the world". On the far left is a water colour by John White depicting an encounter between the English and the Eskimos during an expedition to Greenland. The near left picture shows one of the first maps of North America. Below left is a painting of Sir Walter Raleigh and his son, by an unknown artist. Below, two water-colours by John White depict the village life of the American Indians. After Virginia, Bermuda and Newfoundland were colonized.

The miniature reproduced above shows the poet William Teshe in the act of presenting the manuscript of his book Elizabeth and Fame *to the Queen, who rides in her triumphal carriage guided by a winged Fame. It is to be hoped that in real life the sumptuous carriage of the English queen had more comfortable wheels. The inscription reads: "The rich show gold/The soldier feats of war/The schoolmen art/The lawyer pleads at bar/ O noble Queen/poor Teshe presents his art and prays your grace/to take it in good part." On the left is a picture of the castle of Sir Thomas Lucy at Charlecote, near Stratford, in whose grounds Shakespeare is said to have poached venison. On the right: Sir Thomas' tomb.*

# SHAKESPEARE LEAVES STRATFORD

London was the great attraction for the young of those days as well as for those in search of their fortune. For a clever and brave young man who lived less than a hundred miles away it must have been irresistible. Shakespeare had probably by now come to the conclusion that he would achieve nothing by staying in Stratford. He was no doubt one of those young men who perplex their elders by wanting to make their own way in life; also, he was, at twenty, married with three children and still without a trade, though he had presumably tried many. Although there is no proof, legend has it that Shakespeare's love of hunting was eventually responsible for his sudden departure for London. Near Stratford were the Charlecote woods which were full of deer and game. This land belonged to Sir Thomas Lucy and he employed a number of game-keepers to discourage poachers. On one occasion Shakespeare is said to have been caught poaching and Sir Thomas then threatened him with imprisonment. The young man's reply was a satirical ballad which so amused his companions and so infuriated the baronet that Shakespeare decided the time had come for a change of air. Proud as he was, with a great sense of justice, the poet never forgot the insult and many years later when he wrote *The Merry Wives of Windsor* he created the character of Justice Shallow whose coat-of-arms, like Sir Thomas Lucy's, had a foreground of pike. A Welsh parson in the play marvellously bungles the word "luces" which he pronounces as "louses". Whether this legend of Shakespeare's enforced departure is true or not, there would have been good reason enough for a man interested in the theatre and in writing to make his way to London, which was then much more the centre of English creative activity than it is today. Five companies of travelling players passed through Stratford in 1587, all of them based in London. There were, too, the publishers, and among them a man who himself came from Stratford, William Field. He was not much older than Shakespeare, whose plays show that he must have been familiar with Field's publications. London also was the scene of the exciting preparations for the threatened invasion of the Spanish Armada. A year before that invasion, one morning in 1587, the poet finally took his leave of Stratford, and set out on the road to London.

The "Young Elegant" by Nicholas Hilliard presents an attractive picture of Elizabethan gentility. On the right is a portrait of the English poet and dramatist George Chapman (1559-1634), taken from his translation of Homer's Iliad which he completed in 1611, and which was the subject of a famous sonnet by Keats.

# EVEN A SHORT JOURNEY WAS AN ADVENTURE

From one town on the river to another. The journey from Stratford on the Avon to London on the Thames was not a long one; on horseback, the customary method of travel in those days, it would have taken the poet two or three days of leisurely travel, stopping at village inns and perhaps spending the hotter hours of the day in a cool wood. The English countryside was sparsely populated in those days and covered in forests and woods. On the estates of the wealthy old mansions stood out, bearing the scars of the last ten years of civil war. But already new dwellings were being built, no longer for war but for the country residences of the upper classes. Travellers journeyed by coach or on horseback, and preferably in groups for safety—as the forests were full of rogues eager to cut both throats and purse strings. A journey, however short, was an adventure during which anything might happen. Many of Shakespeare's works echo this feeling of unreality in connection with journeys, repeating the theme of men wandering through woods —rogues, political exiles, exiled kings, innocent people wrongfully accused and obliged to take flight, unhappy lovers or people as strange as the Athenians in *A Midsummer Night's Dream* not to mention Titania and Oberon and all the fairies who figure in that comedy. In the inns at night travellers exchanged tales in which it was difficult to distinguish the real from the supernatural. Mental attitudes still retained much that was medieval, and the belief in witches and fairies was shared by all. Such fantasies were everywhere—in serious drinking, in coarse jokes, in quarrels, in love. The English in this second half of the century, well on the way to their Renaissance, were a gay, full-blooded, curious and violent people, determined to enjoy life to the full without being worried by too many scruples. The favourite forms of entertainment were fights between chained bears and bulls, and mastiffs; public hanging, drawing and quartering; and last but not least, the theatre, which had begun to develop along new lines, discarding the old morality play and offering dark tragedies full of bloodthirsty scenes, such as *The Spanish Tragedy* by Thomas Kyd (1557-95), one of whose lost plays may have influenced Shakespeare's *Hamlet*.

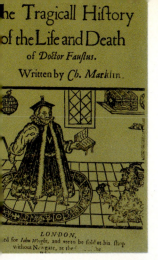

The Tragicall History of the Life and Death of *Doctor Faustus*. Written by *Ch. Marklin*.

LONDON,
...ed for *John Wright*, and are to be fold at his fhop without Newgate, at the ...

Hiftory of the two Maids of More-clacke.

VVith the life and fimple maner of IO H N in the Hofpitall.

Played by the Children of the Kings Maiefties Reuels.

VVritten by *Robert Armin*, feruant to the Kings moft excellent Maieftie.

LONDON,
Printed by N.O. for *Thomas Archer*, and is to be fold at his fhop in Popes-head Pallace, 1 6 0 9.

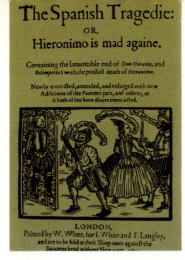

The Spanish Tragedie:
OR,
Hieronimo is mad againe.

Containing the lamentable end of *Don Horatio*, and *Belimperia*; with the pitifull death of *Hieronimo*.

Newly corrected, amended, and enlarged with new Additions of the *Painters* part, and others, as it hath at late been diuers times acted.

LONDON,
Printed by W. White, for I. White and T. Langley, and are to be fold at their Shop ouer againft the Sarazens head without Newgate. ...

*From left to right: the frontispiece of* Doctor Faustus *by Marlowe; a page from another play,* The Two Maids of Moreclack, *with a print of the actor Robert Armin; and the frontispiece from* The Spanish Tragedy *by Kyd, one of the gloomiest of Elizabethan dramas, featuring a bloodthirsty series of murders which none of the characters survives.*

*Above: a painting of the Flemish school showing the Thames at Richmond in the early seventeenth century. In the background can be seen the towers of the royal castle; in the foreground town and country folk are out walking by the river. On the far left, the poet George Gascoigne, crowned by a laurel wreath, offering a manuscript to the Queen. The near left picture shows Englishwomen's fashions in the sixteenth century. Commerce and industry were developing during the latter part of the century. In 1590, when Shakespeare presented his first work, the metallurgical industry already had 7,000 paid workers.*

# A LONDON PULSATING WITH LIFE

The places of entertainment in the capital were south of the river at Banke Side. The city was spread out on the north bank of the Thames, down to the water's edge. The houses were tall and narrow with red pointed roofs. From Banke Side the expanse of roof tops seemed to be bristling with spires, towers and steeples and above them all towered the grey mass of St. Paul's Cathedral. A little further down stands the Tower of London, dark with its unhappy memories of past and present. The maps of the time show us a great mass of buildings interspersed by narrow streets whose names are the same to this day—Cheapside, White Chapel, Lombard Street, Aldgate . . . The oldest part of the town was surrounded by a long wall which ran from Blackfriars in a great

arc back to the river at the royal stronghold of the Tower. The city itself had expanded far beyond those boundaries and stretched into rapidly growing suburbs and green countryside. A solitary gigantic bridge spanned the river, London Bridge. It appeared more like a street built over the river than a bridge; along either side of it were rows of houses, as high as those on the land but huddled still more closely together. The Thames was always full of sailing ships of every kind and every flag, and traffic reached a peak of activity during high tide. In the streets of London the crowds were varied and picturesque—cavaliers in their sumptuous velvet clothes, perhaps rather out of keeping with the swords at their sides, mixed with the tradesmen leaving their shops to greet their customers, and with the merchants travelling to and from the ports about their business. The streets were narrow and none too clean and the maze of blind alleys and tiny lanes remains one of London's oldest characteristics. The shops were often roomy and elegant, like those which were opened in the arcade under the Royal Exchange. The building had been finished shortly before Shakespeare's arrival in London. The City of London was in fact the pulsating heart of a country now fully awakened. A new way of life was being born, together with a new philosophy.

Above: a view of London as it was in the late sixteenth century. The great mass of the town can be seen on the north bank of the river and opposite on Banke Side, where most places of entertainment were to be found, among them the rings for bull and bear baiting. The city was in full growth and by the first half of the century, at the beginning of Elizabeth's reign, numbered some 50,000 inhabitants over the wider area of suburban London. By the end of the century the population had doubled in number. England had at that time a population of 5,000,000. On the left is the print of Queen Elizabeth which appears on the face of the document of the Great Seal for Ireland. On the far left, bakers are seen at their trade.

Below: the great eighteenth-century actor, Garrick, in Richard III. *This difficult role of a deformed and vicious king was his greatest challenge. On the right is a portrait of Henry Carey, the first Baron Hunsdon. He was Lord Chamberlain and owned the company in which Shakespeare worked. Opposite, above: a page* from Titus Andronicus. *Below is the frontispiece from a chronicle by E. Halle which Shakespeare used as a source for his histories; and a page from the* Book of Sir Thomas Moore, *a comedy which Shakespeare wrote with the help of others. The few surviving examples of his hand show that he used the old-fashioned Gothic script.*

# FIRST ENCOUNTER WITH BURBAGE'S THEATRE

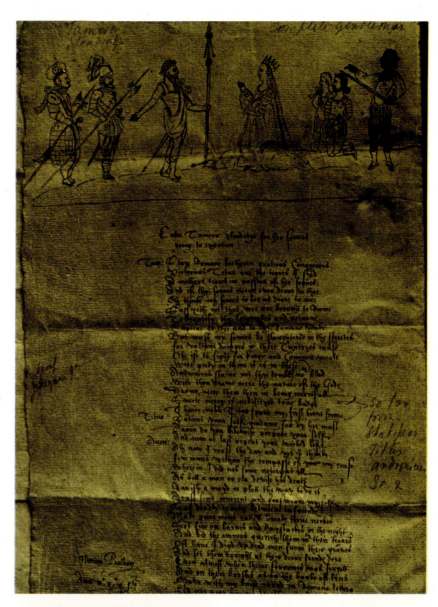

Of Shakespeare's first years in London we know hardly anything. Our first clue is in 1592, when we hear that the son of the glove-maker of Stratford is an actor and playwright of note, with many admirers and some enemies. The five years from his departure from Stratford in 1587 up to 1592 were the years which moulded his temperament and his writing. But what sort of a life did he lead in the capital during these years? In the beginning it was most likely a poor one, as he mixed with people of every kind; but like every well-meaning young man from the provinces he must, before leaving home, have armed himself with letters of introduction to people already in London; this would have been the means by which he made his initial all-important contact with the rich cultured society of the capital. Among them was the printer, Richard Field, who worked for the French publisher Thomas Vautrollier, a fugitive Huguenot and publisher of the works of Calvin and Giordano Bruno. Shakespeare must have absorbed a great deal on a great many subjects, from the translation of the Italian novels by Bandello to Machiavelli's *The Prince,* from the chronicles of the English kings by Ralph Holinshed to all that was written and published by his contemporaries. Tradition has it that during his first weeks in London he earned his living by waiting at the door of the playhouse of James Burbage and holding the horses of those who had no servants. Probably it is more truthful to say that he soon made contact with Burbage and became a trusted friend and fellow actor. James Burbage was a man of considerable importance in London theatrical and literary circles. The leading comedian in the most privileged of all the companies of actors, he was the first to conceive of the idea of building a permanent theatre: this he did in the year 1576. Called simply "the Theatre", it was built in Shoreditch in the centre of London and its existence was the solution to so many problems that it became the prototype of the Elizabethan theatre, the original which inspired all others. The company relied heavily on James Burbage, no longer a young man, and on his sons Richard and Cuthbert. Shakespeare teamed up with them soon after his arrival in London and never left them during his entire career; together they wrote and produced over 30 works.

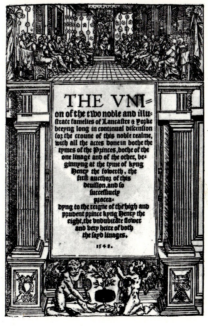

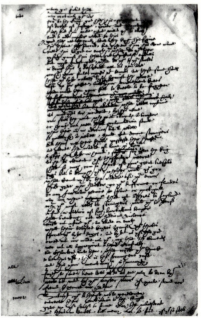

# HIGH-RANKING PATRONS FOR THE PLAYERS

About the year 1590, when Shakespeare had really begun to breathe the air of the capital, the theatre was enjoying a period of great popularity and many new developments were taking place. In the past, performances took place wherever possible—in market squares, in castle halls, in palaces and, mainly, in the courtyards of inns. The players were often little more than groups of vagrants who announced their arrival by noisy fights and brawls. However, little by little after Elizabeth's accession to the throne the theatre became more and more popular and the companies of actors grew in numbers and importance. They were formed into groups which were administered and directed by men of real talent. In 1572 Parliament passed an Act for the Punishment of Vagabonds and only those companies of players who enjoyed the patronage of the nobility were allowed to tour the provinces. The companies took on the names of their patrons and became "Pembroke's Men", "Leicester's Men", "The Lord Admiral's Men" and so on, and with this new-found self-respect the actors gained the sympathy and admiration of the nobility and the common people. When Shakespeare began working in London two rival companies dominated the scene: one was that of James Burbage, under the protection of the Earl of Pembroke, the other had as patron the High Admiral, Lord Charles Howard, and the leading actor was the great Edward Alleyn. Burbage and his men worked at the "Theatre" while Alleyn's company per-

*Left: a portrait of Queen Elizabeth, richly and magnificently dressed, attributed to Nicholas Hilliard. Below: Knights of the Garter, in a painting by Marcus Gheeraerts. Elizabeth stands on the left of the picture, behind her equerry; on the other side stands the Emperor Maximilian of Germany surrounded by members of his court.*

formed at the "Rose", built in 1588, the same year as the great English victory over the "invincible" Armada. Fame spread her wings over England and a happy combination of circumstances prepared the way for the flowering of the English Renaissance. The Queen, first of all, loved the theatre and music. Her court orchestra consisted of eighteen trumpets, seven violins, six flutes, six bagpipes, four drums and a choir of ten. This was a great expense but the Queen knew how to circumvent the protests of her administrators, by simply ignoring them. Many, however, considered the theatre to be a source of sin and corruption, and preachers warned the young to keep away from such places. An outbreak of plague in London was to support their allegation.

*An historian has written that the English of Shakespeare's day most admired gentlemen with an old-fashioned air about them, men such as Philip Sidney. It was, however, Sir Francis Drake whom Englishmen most wished to resemble. Given the duties of "watching" the Spanish coast of America and of working out how to circumnavigate the globe, he combined his exploratory expeditions with pirate raids. His ship's speed and lightness gave him success, and Elizabeth protected him and made him a baronet. He is shown below in a famous portrait (artist unknown) which reveals the intelligent face and ironical half-smile of a man accustomed to having his own way.*

After the victory over the Spanish Armada by the ships of her Majesty, with the help of providential storms, England was enjoying a period of growing wealth. The sea which had in the past isolated and protected her now gave her a supremacy which was to endure and be the cause of her greatness and wealth. It was at this time that the great shipping companies were born, whose peaceful fleets were to bring England an empire. These large sailing vessels sailed the seven seas and returned home laden with precious merchandise from Asia, Africa and America. Less fortunately, they also brought the Black Death. This plague was caused by rats and fleas but the English did not know this. Their ideas as to its origin were somewhat confused, as is shown by this syllogism which was very popular among the Puritans: "The cause of the plague is sin, the cause of sin is the theatre, therefore plainly the cause of the plague is the theatre". In 1592 all public places including theatres were closed. Some companies went into liquidation, others in order to survive left London and went on tours of the provinces. All this misfortune, however, was the cause of some good, for to raise money the companies were obliged to sell part of their repertory to the publishers. Thus works saw the light which had hitherto been entrusted to unreliable copies and the memories of the actors. In those days there was no such thing as copyright—a script was sold to a company for between four and eight pounds and the script then belonged to that company until it was published. Once published, anybody could use it. As it was necessary constantly to add to their repertory, the leading actors were often obliged to content themselves with the re-arranging of old scripts. This was either done by themselves or by an actor with literary talent. Shakespeare, as well as acting, was now revising old scripts and proving himself a great asset to James Burbage. Critics still argue about the dates of Shakespeare's works, but it would appear certain that the following works belong to the first period of his writing: *Henry VI* and, possibly, *Richard III; Titus Andronicus; The Comedy of Errors,* and *Love's Labour's Lost.* All these works reveal influences which different writers had on Shakespeare, and they were based on stories borrowed from others.

After the victory over the Armada theatrical performances on water became very fashionable. The engraving on the left shows the Queen at one such performance. Below are portraits of two of the Court's most eminent men: on the left is William Cecil, first Lord Burghley, principal adviser to Elizabeth for the greater part of her reign, and builder of a number of magnificent palaces. Shakespeare based his character Polonius on him when he wrote Hamlet. On the right is Robert Dudley, Earl of Leicester, and favourite of the Queen. Because of her gifts and her indulgence towards him he managed to become the richest man in England, and one of the most powerful.

# TYPVS ORBIS TERRARVM.

SEPTENTRIO.

TERRA AVSTRALIS NONDVM COGNITA.

MERIDIES.

QVID EI POTEST VIDERI MAGNVM IN REBVS HVMANIS, CVI AETERNITAS OMNIS, TOTIVSQVE MVNDI NOTA SIT MAGNITVDO. CICERO;

*Above is the famous map by Gerard Mercator, "Orbis Terrarum", drawn in 1571. It is the "Projection of Mercator" on which he based the New Map which Shakespeare referred to in* Twelfth Night, *and which still appears, in a more accurate form, in today's atlases. Knowledge of the old world was precise, but this did not prevent Shakespeare from bending geography to suit his purpose, as he did in* The Two Gentlemen of Verona *where the journey from Verona to Milan is made by sea and care must be taken not to miss high tide! However, he is often surprisingly precise, as when he speaks of the boats in public service at Venice—although it is unlikely that he had ever seen France, Italy, or Denmark except in his mind's eye.*

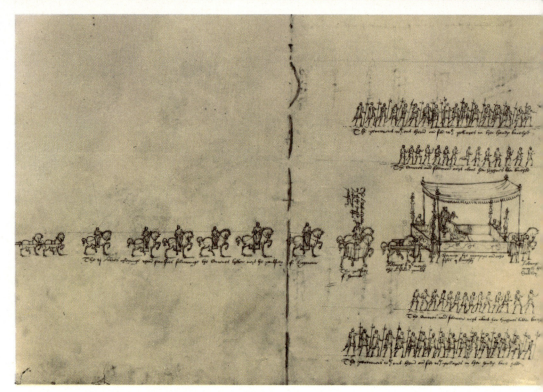

# BORN AT THE RIGHT MOMENT IN HISTORY

Genius will blossom only in the right setting at the right time. Ten years earlier or later, and Shakespeare might never have been what he was. He was born, however, at the right moment in history: England was entering the golden age which waned only with the death of the Queen. The spirit of rebellion of the Reformation blended with the pursuit of pleasure and gaiety so typical of the Renaissance. The English Elizabethans were "a bundle of energy, freed from their old bonds and not yet ensnared in their new"; rejecting old ways of thinking, they turned with a burning curiosity to the new truths through reason. Giordano Bruno visited Oxford in the mid-1580s and gave a lecture on the Copernican theory which refuted the theological view of the universe. The heavens seemed more distant and the earth more real; the rewards of the next life faded when compared with the call of this. Christopher Marlowe, two months younger than Shakespeare, captured the restlessness of the times in his *Doctor Faustus* which he wrote in 1588 and which tells of Faustus's acceptance of damnation to gratify his love of knowledge and power. Marlowe himself followed his character's example by dying at the age of 29 after a life of excesses and depravity. Equally turbulent lives were led by Robert Greene, Thomas Nash, Edmund Spenser, Ben Jonson and many other of their lesser-known companions, who spent much of their time haunting the brothels and the alehouses, or alternatively repenting their sins. Fights and brawls were a daily occurrence, followed perhaps by reconciliations over glasses of Burgundy wine. Poets and dramatists fought each other unscrupulously, spying on and stealing each other's ideas; occasionally they joined forces to fight against actors and managers. Ben Jonson killed a man in a duel; Greene and Kyd died in squalor. Historians have suggested that Marlowe was a government spy, and that his death from stab-wounds was inflicted by another spy. Nevertheless, these men created England's richest and most vigorous literary tradition and they left behind them some of the greatest individual works in the language. Certainly they were much admired in their lifetime, particularly by the aristocracy who, freed from the burden of wars, turned to the world of culture and became patrons of the arts.

*The taste for sumptuous clothes was much in evidence in the reign of Elizabeth. She herself loved to dress spectacularly (on page 32 is a drawing of the procession for her Coronation). Under James I fashion was taken even more seriously. It was at his court that the architect Inigo Jones became such a success. He had been sent by a wealthy patron to study in Italy and introduced into England the love of classical architecture created by such great Italians as Palladio and Sansovino. He designed many palaces and his work was much imitated. For Queen Anne, wife of James I, he designed masks and theatrical costumes. Some of his costume designs can be seen above. The picture on the left shows a young Elizabethan man, painted in 1588, by an unknown artist.*

# THE WAR OF THE POETS

It was inevitable that even Shakespeare would become involved in the "war of the poets", and Robert Greene was the cause. Shakespeare's rise to fame had been sudden and unexpected and it must have been a cause of great annoyance that this virtual amateur was taking bread from the mouths of the professional writers. In a famous libellous pamphlet printed in 1592, Greene, then dying in squalor and misery, openly accused him of treachery: "Be warned," he urged his fellow poets, "... for there is an upstart crow beautified with our feathers, that with his Tygers heart wrapt in a players hide, supposes he is as well able to bombast out a blank verse as the best of you: and being an absolute Johannes Factotum, is in his own conceit the onely Shake-scene in a country ..." Not everyone, however, harboured such bitter jealousy. After Greene's death the publisher responsible for the printing of this pamphlet publicly begged Shakespeare's pardon. It is evident that the poet's fame was growing. The spring of 1593 sees Shakespeare's first signed work—the poem *Venus and Adonis,* dedicated to his famous patron Henry Wriothesley, Third Earl of Southampton. This was the beginning of what was to develop into a deep friendship. A year later, in 1594, Shakespeare published a second poem, *The Rape of Lucrece,* also dedicated to Southampton but this time in a far more friendly manner than the first which had been merely formal and respectful: "The love I dedicate to your Lordship is without end; whereof this pamphlet without beginning is but a superfluous moity. The warrant I have of your honourable disposition, not the worth of my untutored lines makes it assured of acceptance. What I have done is yours, what I have to do is yours, being part in all I have, devoted yours. Were my worth greater my duty would shew greater, meane time as it is, it is bound to your Lordship; To whom I wish long life still strengthened with all happiness." Southampton was delighted with the two poems. They were published by Richard Field, Shakespeare's friend from Stratford, who had married the widow of his famous master, Vautrollier, and taken over the firm. Jacqueline Vautrollier, now Jacklin Field, is thought by some historians to have been the mysterious "dark lady" of the Sonnets, just as the equally mysterious "sweet boy" was the Earl of Southampton. His friendship with Southampton was of great importance in the moulding of the still young poet. On the death of his father, Southampton, then aged eight, had been made a royal ward; he was excessively rich, a graduate of Cambridge University and a favourite of the Queen. It is probable that through him Shakespeare met the famous scholar, John Florio, translator of the *Essais* of Montaigne.

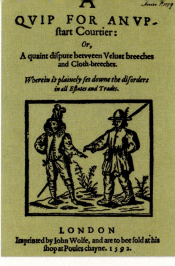

*On the opposite page is a scene from* The Taming of the Shrew *from a nineteenth-century print, between two scenes from an eighteenth-century edition of* King John. The Taming of the Shrew *was one of Shakespeare's first comedies, probably written after* The Comedy of Errors, *his shortest play, and* The Two Gentlemen of Verona.

*On this page are some bibliographical documents of the time. Top left is the frontispiece from the poem* Venus and Adonis, *the first published work of Shakespeare; next to it are the frontispiece from* A Quip For An Upstart Courtier *by Robert Greene, with the ironic subtitle "A quaint dispute between velvet breeches and cloth breeches", and a drawing of the actor Richard Tarlton. The portrait above is of the actor John Lowin, famous during the time of Shakespeare. On the left is a fine portrait of a lady in theatrical costume; we know that Isaac Oliver painted the portrait but of the sitter nothing is known. Oliver was a well-known Elizabethan miniaturist: his signature appears on the right of the portrait.*

# SIR PHILIP, THE WONDER OF HIS AGE

*Educated, intelligent, ambitious and fickle in love, the Countess of Pembroke was one of the most admired women of her day. Sister of Sir Philip Sidney and niece of the Earl of Leicester, the Queen's great favourite, she shone at court almost as brightly as her brother. Here they are shown in portraits by unknown artists. Below: the frontispiece of the pastoral poem* Arcadia *which Sidney wrote at her request, and dedicated to her. He never dared to publish it and on his deathbed ordered that the manuscript be burned; but it was saved, and published in 1598, the year that Shakespeare had his first comedy published under his own name,* Love's Labour's Lost.

Its support of the arts was one of the most admirable features of the Elizabethan court. Firstly the Queen and then, following her example, William Cecil, her Prime Minister, Leicester, her favourite, Sidney, the perfect gentleman, Sir Walter Raleigh, who financed voyages of discovery, the Earl of Southampton, the Earl and Countess of Pembroke and many other members of the aristocracy made it a matter of principle to support actors and poets. They helped in many ways, not just by lending their names but by giving large sums of money and even through personal hospitality. Shakespeare's patron was the Earl of Southampton. Edmund Spenser, author of *The Faerie Queen,* had the support of Sir Philip Sidney. These patrons were a source of encouragement to struggling artists, and were often, as in the case of Spenser, the determining factor that enabled young poets to survive the poverty in which, then as now, they lived. Many of these aristocrats were themselves inspired to write and tried their hand at sonnets, ballads and pastorals, and their attempts were often as good as those of the professionals. A perfect example was the patron and poet Sir Philip Sidney: a gentleman of noble birth, great learning, almost feminine beauty and indomitable courage, he reflects the age most fully, almost to perfection. He travelled all over Europe making friends of philosophers and poets, sat for the painter Veronese and modelled himself on Baldassar Castiglione's "Courtier" and in his turn became the idol of two generations of Englishmen. His sonnets have been considered worthy of comparison with those of Shakespeare. He dedicated his poem *Arcadia* to his sister the Countess of Pembroke, a most cultured and versatile lady, but his greatest poem was his own life. "One can be a poet without writing verse," he wrote, "and write verse without being a poet." He died at the Battle of Zutphen, helping the Dutch to fight the Spanish; the cause of his death was a thigh wound. Edmund Spenser described him as the "wonder of his age" and an historian wrote that though the English were still uncouth in some ways they were trying to become more gentlemanly. He went on to say that he saw in Sidney all the virtues that he himself would like to possess.

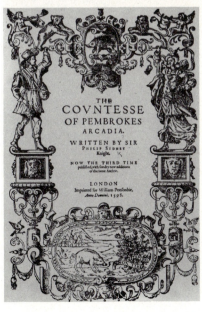

THE COVNTESSE OF PEMBROKES ARCADIA.

WRITTEN BY SIR PHILIP SIDNEI Knight.

NOW THE THIRD TIME published, with sundry new additions of the same Author.

LONDON Imprinted for William Ponsonbie, Anno Domini, 1598.

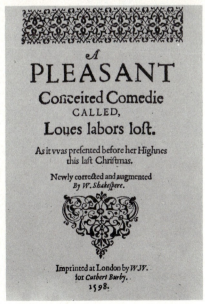

A PLEASANT Conceited Comedie CALLED, Loues labors lost.

As it vvas presented before her Highnes this last Christmas.

Newly corrected and augmented By W. Shakespere.

Imprinted at London by W.W. for Cutbert Burby. 1598.

*Below: an early seventeenth-century print of London Bridge, with its lines of tall houses. A huge melting-pot of old and new ways, London harboured in its underworld men of every conceivable type. The engraving below shows the gap between rich and poor. In 1563, to reduce the number of unemployed and to discourage vagabonds, the Law of Apprenticeship was passed whereby every young man had to serve seven years of apprenticeship because: "A man who has not reached his twenty-third year is nearly always raw and without sense and without the experience to know how to behave". On the opposite page the Lord Mayor of London and his wife are seen in procession.*

# THE WORKINGS OF POWER

The plague, which killed off one-tenth of London's inhabitants, was over. The theatres re-opened and the companies of actors began to reorganize: and, as always happens after a period of suffering, pleasure seemed more desirable than ever. Burbage's company re-opened at the "Theatre" under the protection of Henry Carey, the Lord Chamberlain and Elizabeth's cousin. With such mighty support the actors' position at court, already good, became excellent. On many occasions they performed before the Queen, especially during her birthday celebrations. Among the plays that pleased Elizabeth most was *Love's Labour's Lost,* an elegant little play about love between the King of Navarre and the daughter of the King of France. The dialogue is somewhat stylized and gives the impression of having been written for an audience of aristocrats, as it probably had been. Access to the court gave the young Shakespeare the chance to study at close quarters the life of royalty and politics, in which he was acutely interested. In his plays on the English kings and in many other of his works Shakespeare dwells on the problems which arise from power, their origins, their deviations and their consequences. He was fascinated by the deep and complex relations which tie a prince to his people and to his conscience. Upon this triangle the lives of many of his heroes are based. He admired Elizabeth and she was an inspiration to him when he created his wise and prudent princes. Shakespeare was not ambitious and did not seek to make use of his introduction to court to gain personal favours. Power did not dazzle him, but he must have been affected by the inferior position in which his obscure birth and his being an actor placed him; as his genius developed his plays show an increasing awareness that in rank and position, high or low, lay men's true victories and defeats. He had been in a position to observe both sides of social injustice, and often referred to them in his works: "The oppressors wrong, the proud man's contumely, The pangs of despised love, the law's delay, The insolence of office and the spurns that patient merit of the unworthy takes..." These are the words of Hamlet in his famous speech of Act III, but they are also those of the poet, the voice of the man who has known at close quarters the workings of power, and is left with no illusions.

Lady Mayoress

# THE INN COURTYARD BECOMES A THEATRE

Towards the end of the century London had four or five theatres, all built on the same pattern as the first "Theatre" of James Burbage. This had been modelled on the inns where performances had been mainly held. The inns were rectangular in shape with a courtyard in the centre and a balcony on the second level of the building. Part of the courtyard served as a stage and the remainder was used by standing spectators. If we remember that the normal life of the inn continued during performances with servants and travellers constantly crossing the yard, perhaps stopping a moment to watch or to exchange a witty remark with the actors, we will have some idea of how the Elizabethans looked upon the open theatre. Burbage's theatre retained the rectangular shape of the inn courtyards and the main part of the acting area consisted of a platform stage jutting out into the auditorium, round three sides of which the audience could gather. Trap doors were built into the stage with machinery for raising demons and spectres. A curtained balcony stage served to present balcony scenes, castle battlements, city walls, etc., and was topped by a minstrels' gallery. Above this were dressing rooms and storage for the wardrobe and props. With the help of simple mechanical devices, special theatrical effects could be obtained which were an indispensible part of an Elizabethan production—thunderstorms, hellfire, heavenly music, and so on. The actors had to be very versatile as each had to play different parts in the same play, improvising and turning rapidly from tragic to comic roles.

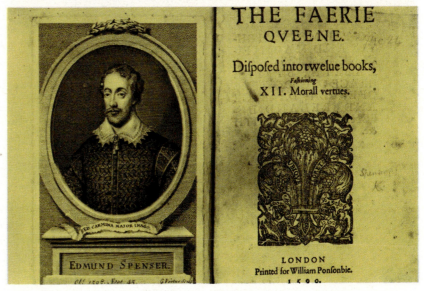

*Three aspects of the Elizabethan theatre: on the opposite page is a model, and the tiny drawing, above left, is of the famous "Globe". The drawing by Johannes de Witt, top right, shows a performance at the "Swan". The round building was reminiscent of the bear-baiting arenas, where bears were made to fight against savage dogs; the rest of the structure was like an inn. Also shown on this page are two poets of the day. Above, far left, is Michael Drayton, another native of Warwickshire, who is supposed to have been Shakespeare's close friend; he wears the wreath of the Poet Laureate. Below is Edmund Spenser and the frontispiece of his poem,* The Faerie Queene. *The work should have comprised twelve volumes, each one dedicated to a different virtue, but Spenser stopped work on it after the sixth volume; even so it is twice as long as the* Iliad.

# AN EXPERIENCED ACTOR

To hold the public's attention from the beginning of a performance was a difficult task. The spectators, even those of the court, chattered, nibbled, played cards, exchanged jokes, played pranks and discussed the happenings on the stage in a loud voice. On the other hand the public was also expected to imagine what was not there—scenery and background for instance. A placard carried by a boy was the only indication of where the action was taking place. There were few props: a tree, a throne or perhaps a table would be carried in and out in full view of the audience. The public had also to accept that female parts tended to be unrealistic since, as is well known, they were at that time played by young boys whose voices had not yet broken. The players' repertory was vast and the players, forced to fight for their public and to distract their attention from their competitors, changed the posters every few days; obviously the quality of the performances was not always of the highest, as they often used old scripts re-hashed and joined haphazardly together, the words improvised by the actors as they went along. Announcing the arrival of the players, Polonius in *Hamlet* says: "The best actors in the world either for tragedy, comedy, history, pastoral, pastoral-comical, historical-pastoral, tragical-historical, tragical-comical-historical-pastoral, scene individable, or poem unlimited." Shakespeare knew the theatre well. We must not forget that he was by profession an actor and that was what he was considered by his contemporaries. He was probably not a great actor but he enjoyed a certain amount of acclaim and his name comes first on the posters of many plays; and even in this often ill-rewarded profession he managed to acquire a small fortune. We have evidence that he played the role of the good servant Adam in *As You Like It* as well as the ghost in *Hamlet;* it seems that the latter role was a great challenge to him. He must have played many other parts, not only in his own plays, since Burbage's repertory included the works of many authors. His name heads the cast in a production of *Every Man in His Humour* by Ben Jonson. After 1594 he was no longer a paid actor but he and the three Burbages were shareholders in the company. The Lord Chamberlain's company was playing to full houses and making handsome profits.

Four vigorous portraits of four outstanding Elizabethan actors: William Sly, Nathan Field, Richard Burbage and Edward Alleyn. That of Burbage is a self-portrait, but the painters of the others are not known. The first three are members of Shakespeare's company, as can be seen from the list of actors, below, which was included in the first edition of Shakespeare's works, published in folio after the poet's death. In the list are other outstanding names such as those of John Heming and Henry Condell, who revised this edition. Edward Alleyn was the leading actor of the rival company (the Lord Admiral's); he created the leading roles in many of Marlowe's plays.

Workes of William Shakespeare,
ntaining all his Comedies, Histories, and
Tragedies: Truely set forth, according to their first
*ORIGINALL.*

### The Names of the Principall Actors
in all these Playes.

| | |
|---|---|
| Illiam Shakespeare. | Samuel Gilburne. |
| Richard Burbadge. | Robert Armin. |
| n Hemmings. | William Ostler. |
| ugustine Phillips. | Nathan Field. |
| liam Kempt. | John Underwood. |
| omas Poope. | Nicholas Tooley. |
| rge Bryan. | William Ecclestone. |
| nry Condell. | Joseph Taylor. |
| liam Slye. | Robert Benfield. |
| hard Cowly. | Robert Goughe. |
| n Lowine. | Richard Robinson. |
| nuell Crosse. | John Shancke. |
| lexander Cooke. | John Rice. |

# JULIET IS BORN

After the Plague had died down in England, Shakespeare enjoyed several years of spiritual and physical well-being. He was in his early thirties, had many friends and his fame had spread even as far as the court. In 1594 he bought a share in the Lord Chamberlain's company; this was probably made possible by his patron, the Earl of Southampton. He had an unburdensome family and an undemanding wife who was content to wait for him in Stratford. He visited his home at least once a year; it is also probable that he spent the Plague-years there. His relationship with his wife was lukewarm though there was no definite rift between them. Without doubt he participated in the tumultuous life of his companions; he was summonsed for breach of the peace and his descriptions of tavern life and other places of entertainment are too vivid to be other than first-hand experiences. In the late seventeenth century, before the romantic legends about him started, much information concerning his private life could still be gathered and formed into a composite portrait. The impression that emerges is that of a pleasant man, quick-witted and a marvellous companion. During these years he wrote his lightest, happiest pieces, *The Taming of the Shrew, A Midsummer Night's Dream* and the exquisitely romantic *Romeo and Juliet.* The gaiety and vivacity of many of the characters he created suggest his own great happiness. Puck is as scintillating as a comet, and as ephemeral. Juliet is no languid, weeping heroine, as she has so often been portrayed, but a brave young girl, high-spirited and determined to have her own way, in fact very much a modern figure. *A Midsummer Night's Dream,* which brims over with happiness and fun in every line, is a delicious fantasy about love. There is no doubt that Shakespeare enjoyed these years of his life in London and it is striking that the only authenticated anecdote we have of him shows him in an amorous light. Richard Burbage had an appointment with a lady admirer; on reaching her door he knocked and a voice from inside asked who was there. As at that time he was a tremendous success in the role of Richard II, he answered "Richard II!" He then heard Shakespeare's voice from inside reply, "Good! Then tell Richard II that William the Conqueror got here first."

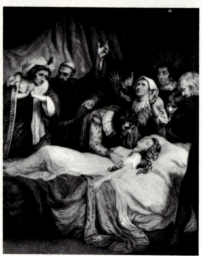

*Above: Juliet's balcony in Verona; according to legend it is here that the two young lovers held their secret meetings. Is it legend or truth? Historians do not believe in its authenticity but their view is not shared by the many young lovers who go there on pilgrimages. Below: two old prints of Shakespeare's* Romeo and Juliet. *Until he later revised it this tragedy contained a bawdy element that seems strange to us today. On the left is Juliet before Romeo's suicide. On the right: the scene in which she kills herself. Opposite: two water-colours by William Blake inspired by* A Midsummer Night's Dream, *which are in the Tate Gallery, London. In the eighteenth and nineteenth centuries Shakespeare's creations were often distorted in a baroque or excessively romanticized manner.*

*Bricklayer and soldier before he became a poet and writer, Benjamin Jonson had a turbulent life. He was sent to prison for killing a man in a duel, but he also enjoyed years of acclaim in literary circles. Below is his portrait and the frontispiece of his* Workes, *the greatest of which is considered to be his comedy* Volpone.

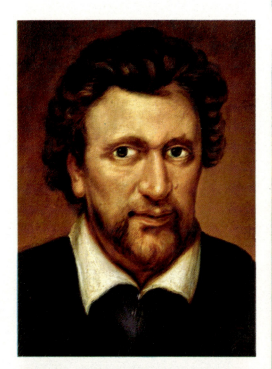

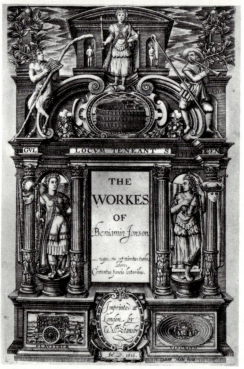

# TWO OR THREE NEW PLAYS EVERY YEAR

Opposite: a full-length painting of the Earl of Southampton, Henry Wriothesley, Shakespeare's patron. Left: a portrait believed to be of Christopher Marlowe, the "damned poet" who was killed in a brawl. Below: a print of 1673 showing popular figures of the time. In the foreground are Sir John Falstaff and Mistress Quickly, from Henry IV.

Circumstances favoured Shakespeare. Towards the end of the century, at the time he was most ready for it, the ground suddenly and tragically cleared and most of the established writers disappeared while the new men were not yet ready to compete. Greene died in 1592, Marlowe in 1593, Kyd in 1594, Peele in 1596. Lyle and Lodge stopped writing for the theatre in 1590. Ben Jonson wrote his first successful comedy in 1599 and George Chapman became famous only after 1600. Shakespeare worked solidly at the rate of two or three plays a year; they were nearly always successes, often outstandingly so. Richard III's cry of "A horse, a horse, my kingdom for a horse", immediately became a popular expression. Before the end of the century Shakespeare had written approximately 20 plays (the order in which they were written is uncertain but we have set them down in the order given by Professor G. B. Harrison, an authority on Shakespeare): the three parts of *Henry VI, Richard III, Titus Andronicus, Love's Labour's Lost, The Two Gentlemen of Verona, A Comedy of Errors, The Taming of the Shrew, Romeo and Juliet, A Midsummer Night's Dream, Richard II, King John, The Merchant of Venice,* the two parts of *Henry IV, Much Ado About Nothing, The Merry Wives of Windsor, As You Like It, Julius Caesar, Henry V, Troilus and Cressida.* They represent an achievement unequalled in the history of literature. Some of the works are undisputed masterpieces but in all of them there are passages of great beauty and an unsurpassed knowledge of acting and the stage. Such abundance can perhaps be explained when one realizes that Shakespeare was not a great scholar intent on polishing verses but a man of the theatre, of whom new scripts were constantly demanded by the eager theatre-goers of London. The poets of his time were prolific writers and do not appear to have been surprised by such an explosion of genius, which stunned later generations and even led some to formulate elaborate theories of different authorship. The most amusing of these relates to Marlowe: suspected of atheism, homosexuality and devil-worship, Marlowe is supposed to have faked his funeral to escape prosecution; he then reappeared some months later with a new identity. The dates would fit this strange hypothesis but that is all that can be said for it.

Changling    Simpleto

Sr I    Falstafe    Hostes    Clause

# A FAMILY COAT-OF-ARMS

*The top picture is of Robert Devereux, second Earl of Essex and favourite of the Queen. After his failure to pacify the rebels in Ireland, his thirst for power led him to the executioner's block. The centre picture is the coat-of-arms that was granted to Shakespeare's father through the intervention of Essex. Above: the documents relating to its concession. They are in the care of the Trustees of Shakespeare's Birthplace in Stratford. Opposite: part of Denis Von Alsloot's painting of a magnificent procession in the Great Square of Brussels (1615) which reveals much about the prevailing taste for spectacles of every kind.*

In Stratford the fortunes of the Shakespeares had been restored thanks to the poet. His parents were still alive and lived in the house in Henley Street with their other children, grandchildren and their daughter-in-law. John Shakespeare, notwithstanding his past adversities, had never lost the esteem of his fellow-citizens but he had one last ambition—the family crest he had wished for all his life. It was his son, William, who obtained it for him—a crest with a falcon brandishing a spear and under it the words "Non sans droict" (Not Without Right) a debatable point as the only record of his ancestors is of one William Sakspere who was hanged for theft in 1248. But in Elizabethan England the rise of the middle classes was an everyday occurrence. Certainly Shakespeare cannot have been displeased to find himself the son of a gentleman. His friend, Ben Jonson, never stopped teasing him about it and wrote a scene in one of his comedies where a person's coat-of-arms bears the head of a boar with the motto "Not without Mustard". In this same summer of 1596 while Shakespeare was touring the provinces with his actors, his only son, Hamnet, died. He was eleven years old. We know nothing of the cause of his death, of which the only existing record is a curt line in the parish register, on the page reserved for deaths: "August 11, Hamnet, filius William Shakespeare". It must have been a terrible blow for the poet to lose this child on whom all his hopes were centred. One of the themes of the Sonnets is the need for children: "For where is she so fair whose unear'd womb Disdains the tillage of thy husbandry? Or who is he so fond will be the tomb of his self-love, to stop posterity?" In his tragedies there is a recurrent theme of innocent children—the young princes who were suffocated in the Tower in *Richard III;* the children of Macduff: "What! all my pretty chickens and their dam, at one fell swoop?"; the young prince Arthur in *King John,* mourned by his mother with touching words: "Grief fills the room up of my absent child, Lies in his bed, walks up and down with me, Puts on his pretty looks, repeats his words, Remembers me of all his gracious parts, Stuffs out his vacant garments with his form". And King Lear, holding Cordelia's body in his arms, cries with anguish: "She's gone forever!"

# SHAKESPEARE'S UNHAPPINESS AT THE DOWNFALL OF ESSEX

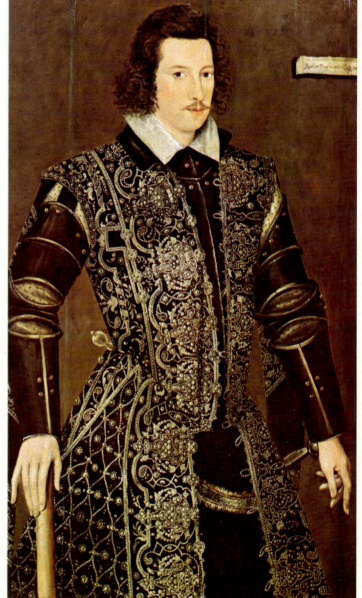

It was Essex's support that secured for Shakespeare his father's coat-of-arms. Robert Devereux, Second Earl of Essex, the Queen's new favourite, had for many years shone like a sun on the London world. Handsome, brilliant, arrogant, proud to the point of conceit, he had taken Sidney's place in the hearts of the people and had also, incidentally, married his widow. His great chance came when Elizabeth sent him to Ireland as Viceroy to combat the rebels. His departure was a glorious one and Shakespeare wished to celebrate in anticipation the victorious return of the handsome Earl (his patron, Southampton, was a close friend of Essex). He set about writing *Henry V,* a poem of national glory in which Shakespeare compares Essex to the victorious young king at Agincourt: "As, by a lower but loving likelihood, Were now the general of our gracious empress,—As in good time he may,—from Ireland coming, Bringing rebellion broached on his sword, How many would the peaceful city quit To welcome him!" But that day never came. Essex made a series of disastrous mis-

takes that quickly led to his downfall. Ruined and disgraced he tried to rouse the people against the Queen. On the eve of the date he had planned, his supporters persuaded Burbage's company to act the allusive play *Richard II,* in which a sovereign is dethroned, but a great deal more would have been needed to overthrow Elizabeth. Essex was captured and tried; he confessed and was executed, and all England mourned him. By 1601 the new century had brought with it a gradual but sensible decline in the quality of life. Even in Shakespeare's works the joyful tone had gone and his outlook on life became pessimistic. The world appeared to him as a huge machine, sinister and impersonal, that brutally crushed man in its mechanism. In the play *Henry VIII* Cardinal Wolsey says: "This is the state of man: today he puts forth The Tender leaves of hope; tomorrow blossoms, And bears his blushing honours thick upon him; The third day comes a frost, a killing frost; And, when he thinks, good easy man, full surely His greatness is a-ripening, nips his root."

For two decades Catholic Ireland, often aided by Spain, had been a thorn in the flesh of Protestant England. Revolt followed revolt and each was ruthlessly crushed. Inhuman massacres took place, such as that on the Isle of Rathlin where 600 Irish, mainly women, children and old men, were put to the sword. Twenty years later Essex tried in vain to crush the Rebellious Irish under their leader The O'Neil, Earl of Tyrone. On the opposite page two scenes of Irish life are shown from the book The Image of Ireland, published in 1581. Next to these is a painting of the Earl of Essex.

The scene in which Falstaff examines the recruits in Henry IV was probably inspired by the preparations for Essex's expedition to Ireland. Above: a painting by Hogarth depicts the assembly of the less able-bodied. On the left is a scene from Richard II. Essex's supporters tried to make use of this play to encourage the people of London to rise against the Queen. Shakespeare did not have to resort to his imagination to write about acts of violence—executions, hangings, duels, massacres, vendettas were not rare occurrences in the tempestuous age of Elizabeth.

*Three scenes from* Julius Caesar: *Anthony's speech to the people, showing them the dead body of Caesar, manages in a few moments to change their mood and to rouse them against the conspirators. It is a perfect example of political psychology. For the writing of this work Shakespeare studied Plutarch's* Lives. *The ancient world* of the Mediterranean attracted him and inspired such works as Titus Andronicus, Coriolanus, *and* Julius Caesar, *which are set in ancient Rome.* Troilus and Cressida *takes place during the siege of Troy. On the other hand,* A Midsummer Night's Dream, Timon of Athens, Pericles *and* A Comedy of Errors *are set in Greece.*

# IN FALSTAFF A PORTRAIT OF THE LORD CHAMBERLAIN

The new Chamberlain, Lord Cobham, who took the place of Lord Hunsdon, was a Puritan, a declared enemy of the theatre and as such refused to give his protection to the company which he had inherited with the post. But Burbage's actors had the sympathy of the Queen, and Shakespeare must have been very sure of himself to dare to attack the Lord Chamberlain with his deadly ridicule. In *Henry IV* he created a fat, witty, debauched, cowardly blusterer—always first at the revels, always last on the battlefield—and he gave him the name of Sir John Oldcastle. As Oldcastle was an ancestor of Lord Cobham, Cobham not unnaturally protested and the name was changed to Falstaff, but by protesting he laid himself open to ridicule, and all London laughed. This part is one of Shakespeare's most lively creations: "that reverend vice, that grey iniquity, that father ruffian, that vanity in years". His pure cynicism: "Can honour set me a leg? No. Or an arm? No. Or take away the grief of a wound? No . . . Detraction will not suffer it. Therefore I'll none of it: honour is a mere scutcheon . . ." And yet he dies of a broken heart when the young Prince of Wales, the companion of his revels, repudiates him after becoming king. Tradition has it that Elizabeth was so pleased with the character of Falstaff that she ordered the poet to show her Falstaff in love, an order which produced *The Merry Wives of Windsor*—written in fifteen days—in which Falstaff is made a fool of by the two merry wives. Shakespeare was now a wealthy man; he bought New Place, the second finest house in Stratford, and two barns and two gardens in the middle of the town. In 1599 Burbage was obliged to leave the "Theatre" as his lease of the land had expired. He, Shakespeare and other actors of the company went into partnership and built a new and larger theatre, the "Globe", most famous of all Elizabethan playhouses, "in the shape of a wooden O". The Globe was to be burned to the ground fourteen years later in a fire caused by gun-shots heralding the opening of a play. The "Globe bore the Latin motto "All the World's a Stage", most probably thought up by Shakespeare. In this theatre his great characters Hamlet, Othello, Macbeth and King Lear were seen for the first time, bringing all the sorrow of the world to its stage, and his passionate doomed heroines declaimed their lines.

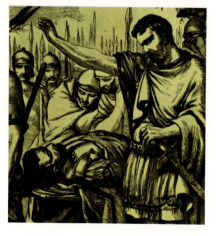

*The final scene in* The Merry Wives of Windsor. *Falstaff, disguised with deer's antlers as Herne the Hunter, discovers that he has been duped by the merry wives with whom he had hoped for an amorous rendevous. Below: the portraits of three English kings who were the subjects of plays by Shakespeare, Henry IV, Henry V and Richard III.*

# SHAKESPEARE'S "SAD YEARS": THE PRICE OF MATURITY

The beginning of the new century, after Essex's death, was the start of what biographers call Shakespeare's "sad years". Gone are the gay, light-hearted comedies and in their place come the tragedies—Hamlet's powerlessness, Troilus' disgust, Othello's despair, Timon of Athens' misanthropy. These words of Macbeth seem to come from the darkest region of Shakespeare's soul: "Life's but a walking shadow, a poor player, That struts and frets his hour upon the stage, And then is heard no more; it is a tale Told by an idiot, full of sound and fury, Signifying nothing". We do not know what happened to him to create this solemnity; we do not even know if it could be traced to actual misfortunes, or if, rather, it formed part of the natural development of a sensitive spirit. His characters now see life as a battle to be fought and won, without the full price that it demands; but victory is seen as almost always impossible. He has compassion for man because he realizes the forces that man, whether he be king or fool, has to fight to save himself from disaster. The germ of self-destruction is within us all, ready to grow as soon as circumstances become favourable. All the actors in his great tragedies are destined for disaster, fighting against it like fish caught in a net, each one tied by a knot of pain, and failing because the real fight is against himself. But the poet neither judges nor condemns them; he remains impartial and understands their human failings. Whatever may have been the cause of Shakespeare's pain, it does not eradicate in him the capacity for love (in its widest sense). From his works, even from those of his saddest years, there emerges the picture of a well-balanced man, sensitive to friendship, music and the pleasures of life; naturally he was sensitive also to pain. Like all those who are capable of great enjoyment he was also capable of great suffering. After 1608, however, his spirit became more calm in an acceptance of his fate, and in this mood *The Tempest* was born. Prospero speaks these words with smiling resignation: "We are such stuff As dreams are made on, and our little life Is rounded with a sleep". Perhaps the enchanted calm achieved in *The Tempest* could have been reached only through the complete exposure of man, stripped of the social trappings which are so much a part of the tragedies.

*Son of the Catholic Mary Stuart, James I married a Catholic, Anne of Denmark, but was himself brought up as a Protestant and defended his faith. Temperamentally he was the opposite of Elizabeth in every way. An historian wrote that the only thing these two had in common was the fact that both their mothers had been beheaded. The miniature below is of Queen Anne; also below is one of the arches of triumph erected for the Coronation of James I, and a print of the Coronation itself. Opposite is a portrait of King James by the artist D. Mytens; accustomed to fend for himself from early childhood, he wore quantities of clothes to protect himself from stab-wounds.*

# JAMES I'S ACCESSION BRINGS HAPPIER DAYS FOR THE THEATRE

After forty-five years of glorious if not always peaceful reign, Elizabeth died. England held her breath, "for when a monarch dies he does not die alone but like a whirlpool sucks down that which has been closest to him". Fortunately the new accession took place without calamity. James VI of Scotland, son of Mary Stuart, became James I of England, thus uniting the two kingdoms, and a triumphal procession from Edinburgh to London brought a new phase in the old rivalry. Shakespeare had not a word for the death of his Queen, but adulation had never been his strong point; he had not indulged in it while Elizabeth was alive, he would not do so now that she lay peacefully in Westminster. Only much later, in *Henry VIII*, did he give Archbishop Cranmer who baptized Elizabeth, a speech of prophetic eulogy. The accession of James I to the throne was to bring happier days for the theatre. In spite of bad health and a rather pedantic and shy disposition the King loved feasting and entertainments; fifteen days after his arrival in London he nominated the Shakespeare-Burbage company the "King's Men". From that point they were welcome at court, and revel followed revel with unprecedented splendour. It was the beginning of the degeneracy of the drama, which was being overtaken in popularity by elaborate masques. Inigo Jones, the great architect, was called upon by the King to design for them. He worked out elaborate palaces which would never be built, and exquisite costumes for the King's wife, Anne. Ambiguity and depravity dominated court life. The King had a passion for beautiful young men; his great delight was drinking in the company of men such as Robert Carr, Earl of Somerset, and George Villiers, Duke of Buckingham, and he encouraged his subjects to indulge in sports and entertainment on a Sunday after attending Divine Service. He himself was a fearless rider and hunter. All this very much annoyed the Puritans but in other respects James I was a religious and devout man. In fact he wrote a ponderous volume of verse and essays which he dedicated to Jesus Christ. Favoured by the King, Shakespeare prospered. His patron, Southampton, who had been imprisoned and condemned to death by Elizabeth for his complicity with Essex, was freed by James I and given one of the highest positions at court.

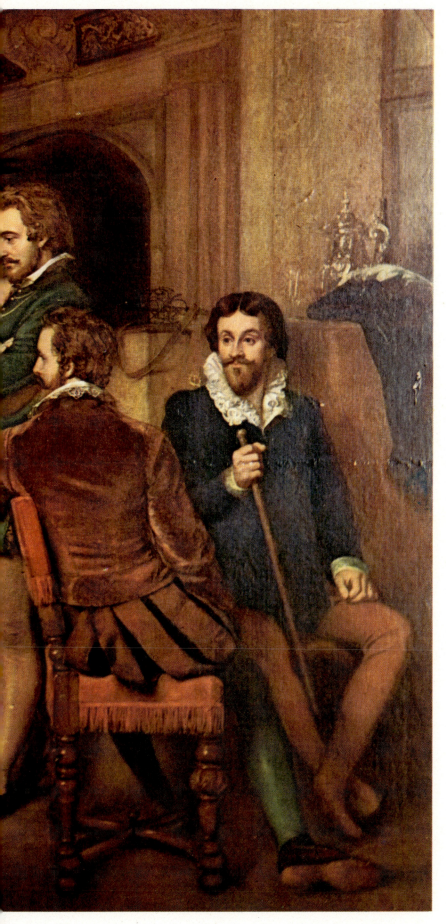

# GAY MEETINGS AT THE MERMAID TAVERN

"What things have we seen done at the Mermaid," wrote Francis Beaumont, the poet and dramatist who was one of the gayest of the writers in London; he maintained that meetings at the famous Mermaid Tavern in Broad Street deserved a poem in their praise. "Heard words that have been so nimble and so full of subtle flame, As if that everyone from whence they came Had meant to put his whole wit in a jest And had resolved to live a fool the rest of his dull life." Among the writers who attended these meetings were William Shakespeare, Ben Jonson, Michael Drayton, George Chapman, John Donne and, of course, Beaumont, whose plays towards the end of the century were even more popular than Shakespeare's. It is possible that their patrons and gentlemen of the court were sometimes present. The taverns were the writers' clubs, the tavern-keepers their friends and confidants from whom they often borrowed money. Shakespeare has described many with his unfailing wit, and we know that these gatherings did not consist of the composed gentlemen that the nineteenth-century painters would have us suppose. Obscene jokes were very popular at the time and the type of women who frequented the taverns were not the sort to have been shocked by them. Many of the poets squandered the money they earned and went from debt to debt. Brawls broke out with startling frequency, heads were smashed, regrets expressed the following day, and then the whole thing begun again. To give them their due, the writers of the Mermaid Tavern also played games of dice and discussed books and philosophy, and waited avidly for news from abroad.

*In this purely imaginary picture Shakespeare is surrounded by his friends, among whom we can identify Ben Jonson, Sir Walter Raleigh and the Earl of Southampton. They are all very pensive, their poses noble and refined—moods and postures different from the real gatherings of these wits and learned men, and giving in combination an annoying impression of lack of spontaneity and truth.*

# THE CHARACTERS OF THE TRAGEDIES ARE CRUSHED BY THEIR FATE

We know nothing of Shakespeare's method of working but he must have had great powers of concentration to achieve such an output. Certainly the fact he had regularly to produce new plays for the stage must have been a stimulus; that he did not have much time to spend polishing his works has contributed to the liveliness of his characters and their theatrical effectiveness. In the ten years between 1600 and 1610 he wrote fifteen plays, most of them tragedies: *The Merry Wives of Windsor, A Midsummer Night's Dream, Hamlet, All's Well that Ends Well, Troilus and Cressida, Othello, Measure for Measure, Macbeth, King Lear, Timon of Athens, Pericles, Antony and Cleopatra, Coriolanus, Cymbeline* and *The Tempest*, followed by *A Winter's Tale* and finally *Henry VIII* which was only partially written by him. In the tragedies he carried to an extreme his analysis of human destiny, seeing man more and more tied to forces beyond his control: the forces of his passions and those of life which are often expressed through nature. There is always a dramatic conflict between the characters and the Cosmos in which he underlines the fact that man belongs to something far greater than himself: "As flies to wanton boys, are we to the gods," says King Lear, and Hamlet states: "There are more things in heaven and earth, Horatio, Than are dreamt of in your philosophy". Othello measures his love for Desdemona in cosmic dimensions: "But I do love thee! and when I love thee not, Chaos is come again". And later in despair at having killed her: "Methinks it should be now a huge eclipse Of sun and moon, and that the affrighted globe Should yawn at alteration". In *Macbeth*, nature is turned upside down when Macbeth kills the king, and unnatural events accompany him on his bloodthirsty rise and fall. "For I am as constant as the Northern Star . . ." says Julius Caesar, little knowing that the star is about to fall. This awareness of the involvement of a human destiny with the universe leads Shakespeare to a religiousness not to be judged in terms of Catholicism or Protestantism but in an awareness of the existence of God—a Being whom he does not mention by name but whose might he recognizes. Hamlet found peace only in resignation: "There's a special providence in the fall of a sparrow. If it be now, 'tis not to come."

On this page are four scenes from
Othello. Shakespeare borrowed the
theme for this play from an existing
story. In his profession, where the
need was not so much to write
masterpieces as to produce
successful plays for the company,
old texts were remodelled and
brought up to date, and pieces were
sometimes lifted from other people's
plays. Many great actors have
played the part of Othello, from
Burbage to Edmund Kean, near left,
from Salvini to Orson Welles and
Laurence Olivier. The role of
Desdemona was the first to be
played on the English stage by a
woman, in 1660. This was the
famous interpretation by Mrs
Siddons, seen above.

# THE GUNPOWDER PLOT

*Of the three sons of James I, Henry Prince of Wales, was the heir, but died prematurely, leaving the throne to his brother Charles who became Charles I. James's daughter, Elizabeth, married King Frederick of Bohemia. Opposite are miniatures of King James, Queen Anne, Prince Henry, King Frederick, Prince Charles and Princess Elizabeth.*

*Even under James I there were victims of fanaticism. Below are three prints of the Gunpowder Plot: a meeting of the conspirators; their being dragged through Parliament Square, and their death by hanging, drawing and quartering. The many English Catholics loyal to the crown suffered greatly from the repressions which followed the Plot.*

At about the time when King James acceded to the throne, there was an increase in emigration to the colonies in America. Country folk ambitious to have their own land, adventurers prepared to try anything that might make their fortune, criminals evading justice, Puritans anxious to breathe an air less polluted with sin, all braved dangers and risked drowning on the three-month voyage to settle in the new England across the sea. After the discovery of Virginia came Bermuda and Newfoundland, and England reached out even as far as Asia under the flag of the East India Company. James was a peaceful man, and he succeeded in keeping the peace for 16 years in spite of Parliament's constant incitement to intervene in the various religious wars that there troubling Europe, and in particular to help Germany in the Thirty Years' War. He resisted and adroitly arranged an alliance with Catholic Spain through the proposed marriage of his son, Charles, to the Infanta. This marriage came to nothing and the Prince's visit to Spain had the sole advantage of acquiring for the royal family a beautiful collection of paintings by Titian. The King loved art, in his own way, just as he loved banquets and drinking parties. He believed implicitly in witches (as did all his subjects) and when still James VI of Scotland had written an imposing treatise on the subject of demonology in which he listed the powers of witches with undeniable and considerable competence. As king of England he became less zealous on the subject; nevertheless crowds still continued their sadistic enjoyment of watching witches burnt at the stake. But the greatest trial of his reign was that of the Gunpowder Plot, a conspiracy to blow up the Houses of Parliament at the opening of Parliament when the King, the royal family, the lords and the commons would be assembled. The conspirators were Catholics and the plot was kept secret for 18 months while a tunnel was dug under the Houses of Parliament and 36 barrels of gunpowder placed in the cellar under the House of Lords. The secret leaked out and the plot was uncovered on the eve of the date fixed. The conspirators were tried and condemned to death. The Jesuit Father Provincial in England was also involved and condemned to death, and so ended the King's dream for a reconciliation between the Catholics and Protestants.

# HE WRITES MACBETH IN PRAISE OF THE SCOTTISH KING

Shakespeare wrote *Macbeth* in honour of the Scottish King; it was the shortest of his tragedies, a tale of ambition, hallucination and witches with the wind-blown Scottish heath as its background. James considered himself to be a descendant of Banquo, the Scottish general of whom the three witches prophesy that he shall be the progenitor of those "which shall governe the Scottische Kingdome by long order of continuall descent". This was, in fact, what happened to Mary Stuart who had died without achieving her ambition to rule England, but by an irony of history was the mother of the new king. The drama was presented at court during the period of festivities held in honour of the visit of James's brother-in-law, King Christian IV, to England. The year was 1606, and ever since *Macbeth* has tempted the greatest actors. Perhaps more than any other of Shakespeare's histories *Macbeth* draws us by its evil fascination as the Scottish thane and Lady Macbeth perform their dark and sinister murder. Shakespeare's career continued without setback as, loved and honoured, he became increasingly the country gentleman. In Stratford, where Shakespeare's father had died happy with his coat-of-arms, the poet now owned a large house and land. In 1607 three events occurred: a writ from the Court of Record against John Addenbrook, a gentleman of Stratford, who for some time had owed Shakespeare the sum of six pounds; the death of his brother Edmund, and the marriage of his first born and favourite daughter, Susanna, to one of the most eligible young men of the town, Dr. John Hall. The following year his mother, Mary Arden, died. It is strange that there remains no reference to her of any kind, not even a portrait of her. Shakespeare, who was then a shareholder of the "Globe" theatre participated with other members of his company in the purchase of the "Blackfriars", a much smaller theatre which catered for a small, select audience. The plays presented there were often masques with music, very much in vogue at the time. The texts became more lyrical and the plots more unrealistic and audiences dwindled. Shakespeare's writings were greatly influenced by the changing times, *The Tempest,* in particular. The Golden Age was at an end and that of Baroque had begun.

David Garrick, left, was considered to be one of the greatest performers in the role of King Lear. Lower left: Ellen Terry, an equally great Lady Macbeth. Lower right: another scene from Macbeth, in which the two Scottish Generals meet the three witches, taken from an illustration in the Chronicles of Ralph Holinshed, one of Shakespeare's principal sources. For the poet the confines between life and death are fluid, separated by sleep. The borders of madness and sanity are as indefinite. Hamlet's feigned madness destroys Ophelia; Lear finds refuge in madness from an unbearable reality; Lady Macbeth (pictured below by Fuseli) loses her sanity under the burden of sin.

# THE SO-CALLED "TRUE" SHAKESPEARES

Not one of Shakespeare's contemporaries would have dreamed of doubting either his identity or the authorship of his works. Those who knew him well are full of praise and precise references to these. In 1598 Francis Meres in his *Palladis Tamia* (Wits Treasury) describes Shakespeare as the finest English author of comedies and tragedies: "If the Muses wished to speak in English they would speak in the finely chisled style of sweet Shakespeare". It was only in the middle of the nineteenth century that a Miss Delia Bacon, American descendant of the great philosopher Sir Francis Bacon, voiced her conviction that Sir Francis, a contemporary of Shakespeare, used the name of Shakespeare to disguise his true identity, but she gave no reason for her ancestor's desire for anonymity. Although Miss Bacon ended her days in a mental home her idea germinated and bore even stranger fruits: a succession of men were now called the "true" Shakespeare—the Earl of Rutland, the Earl of Derby, the Earl of Oxford and a group of writers among whom was even the Countess of Pembroke, presumably as an expert on the female characters. All these theories have been rejected by serious scholars. Bacon's masterpiece, the *Novum Organum,* which introduces scientific methods to the existing philosophy, is on a totally different mental plane from that of Shakespeare's magical and visionary writing. In spite of the great variety of subjects on which Shakespeare wrote, his work has an individuality and quality all its own. His vocabulary is exceptionally rich, comprising some 15,000 words, probably the richest in all the whole of English literature, containing expressions taken from the sea, hunting heraldry, and a thousand other trades and pastimes. All this raw material is made use of by a great imagination which conjures up pictures, many of which have become part of the universal heritage: "Frailty, thy name is woman"; "the devil can cite Scripture for his purpose"; "the milk of human kindness"; "the winter of our discontent". Embellished phrases and precious adjectives were the taste of the period but Shakespeare was able to rise above preciousness with the turn of phrase which is "right". How many of his lines are addressed to the moon; yet on each occasion Shakespeare appears to recreate the vision with freshness and beauty.

Opposite: a painting of Sir Francis Bacon, Lord Verulam, Viscount St Albans, Queen's chancellor, writer and philosopher, and an acknowledged genius. In spite of all this the hypothesis that he was the author of the works of Shakespeare, and the ingenious claims concerning cryptic messages from Bacon in the texts of the plays, hardly merit serious attention. Left: a portrait of Robert Carr, Earl of Somerset, one of James I's favourites. Below: an engraving dated 1613 of Prince Charles presenting the King and Queen of Bohemia to Parliament. Relations between James I and Parliament were often stormy and paved the way for the Civil War and the execution of his son, Charles I.

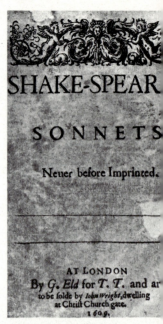

In praise of Willobie his Auisa, Hexameton to the Author.

IN Lauine Land though Liuie boft,
There hath beene feene a Conftant dame:
Though Rome lament that fhe haue loft
The Gareland of her rareft fame,
    Yet now we fee, that here is found,
    As great a Faith in Englifh ground.

Though Collatine haue deerely bought,
To high renowne, a lafting life,
And found, that moft in vaine haue fought,
To haue a Faire, and Conftant wife,
    Yet Tarquyne pluckt his gliftering grape,
    And Shake-fpeare, paints poore Lucrece rape.

PARTHENIA
or
THE MAYDENHEAD
of the first musicke that
euer was printed for the VIRGINALLS.
COMPOSED
By three famous Mafters: William Byrd, Dr. Iohn Bull, & Orlando Gibbons Gentlemen of his Mats. moft Illuftrious Chappell.
Ingrauen by William Hole.
for DOROTHE EVANS
Cum Priuilegio

Printed at London by G. Lowe and are to be fould
at his houfe in Loathbery.

SHAKE-SPEAR

SONNETS

Neuer before Imprinted.

AT LONDON
By G. Eld for T. T. and ar
to be folde by Iohn Wright, dwelling
at Chrift Church gate.
1609.

# THE "FAIR YOUTH" AND THE "DARK LADY" OF THE SONNETS

The central mystery in Shakespeare's life is to be found in the 154 *Sonnets* which were published in 1609 (most probably without the author's consent). They form a collection of lyrics whose burning passion has rarely been equalled in literature. The theme of the *Sonnets* is love and betrayal, and two people are involved—firstly a "fair youth", a young man of great beauty to whom the writer shows a devoted affection. The second is the "dark lady" who ensnares him but, faithless in love, abandons the poet for his young friend. Who were these two people? As far as the man is concerned the Earl of Southampton or the Earl of Pembroke are the most likely candidates. There is much in favour, and much against, either theory, as scholars have found after much research. The dedication in the first edition refers to a "Mr. W. H." as "the only begetter" of the *Sonnets*. Southampton's name was Henry Wriothesley and he was Shakespeare's patron and friend, at least from the time of *Venus and Adonis;* he was young (nine years younger than the poet) but not particularly handsome. It was, however, the fashion of the time to praise the beauty of a person whom one loved or admired, even where it did not exist, as was the case with Queen Elizabeth. The argument in favour of the Earl of Pembroke is not easily dismissed; his name was William Herbert and he was even younger than Southampton, extremely dissolute but a generous patron of the arts. The hypothesis in favour of Pembroke would also fit the "dark lady", for we know that Mary Fitton, the Queen's maid, was Pembroke's mistress. She was a dark beauty and though there is not a shred of evidence to substantiate it, it is not to be denied that Shakespeare, who had friends among the aristocracy and was himself a frequent visitor to the court, might have desired her. Others have suggested that Jacklin Field, wife of the printer already mentioned, was the lady of the *Sonnets*. Whoever the people concerned may have been, the *Sonnets* are Shakespeare's spiritual biography, and from them emerges the profile of a most sensitive spirit able to express every shade of passion from the platonic admiration of a friend to the torments of jealousy, from gay lightheartedness to deepest sorrow, from sensual ecstasy to darkest repugnance.

*Opposite, above: frontispiece of the first complete edition of the dramatic works of Shakespeare, the famous 'first folio' of 1623, containing 36 plays of which only* Othello *had been published before; a citation of the poet's name in the folio; a book of music composed by the chapel masters of the Queen for the virginals, and the frontispiece of the* Sonnets, *published in 1609. Below: a painting by Jan Brueghel the Elder, showing English country people attending a theatrical performance in the village square. This page: Mary Fitton, maid of honour to Elizabeth, in all the splendour of the richest of Elizabethan costumes; could she have been the "dark lady" of the* Sonnets, *Shakespeare's "worser spirit"?*

In 1613 London celebrated the marriage of the King's daughter (the gracious Princess Elizabeth) to the younger Frederik V, Elector Palatine, later to be King of Bohemia. During the period of fesitivity The Tempest was performed at court. Below: the bride and groom and the marriage procession which wound through the streets of London. Opposite: a sermon in St. Paul's Cathedral in the year 1616 (the same year Shakespeare died). The Cathedral was destroyed in the Great Fire of 1666, and this painting gives us a good idea of what it looked like in the time of James I. The artist has ingeniously tried to show the inside and the outside in one picture.

# THE END OF SHAKESPEARE'S THEATRICAL CAREER

Just as we have no precise information about when Shakespeare began his career in London, we know little about when it came to an end. All we do know is that around the year 1610 he broke his ties with the theatre and settled in Stratford, limiting his visits to London to brief business trips. He was now nearly 50 years old, and though his health is believed to have been good, 30 years of intense work and emotional strain must have taken their toll. Stratford attracted him with its memories of the past and the comforts of the present, and there it was he retired in peace to write the three masterpieces of his later years: *Cymbeline, A Winter's Tale* and *The Tempest*. His large house was surrounded by a garden which must have been full of the English flowers he had so often and so lovingly described. At that time also, a grand-daughter was born, the child of Susanna and John Hall, to rekindle his long-standing delight in children; *A Winter's Tale* is filled with this affection. Shakespeare's last work, *Henry VIII,* was only partially written by him, and was produced at the "Globe". It contains a posthumous eulogy to Queen Elizabeth: "Peace, plenty, love, truth, terror, That were the servants to this chosen infant, Shall then be his, and like a vine grow to him". It is a picture he describes as if it were part of his own experience. The days passed serenely until, in July 1613, bad news came from London that the "Globe" Theatre had been burned to the ground. During a performance of *Henry VIII,* the gun-shots heralding the opening of a scene set fire to the thatched roof and in two hours the "round wooden O" had been burned to the last stick of wood. A new "Globe" was built, once again with Shakespeare as a shareholder, but there is no doubt whatsoever that Shakespeare never performed there, and perhaps he did not even visit the new theatre. At the beginning of 1616, which was the last year of his life, Thomas Quiney, a business man of Stratford, asked for the 30-year-old Judith's hand in marriage. His father, Richard Quiney, had previously asked Shakespeare for a loan of £30, in the only surviving letter to Shakespeare, written in 1598. The wedding took place on February 10. Five weeks later Shakespeare made his will: "I, William Shakespeare, gentleman . . ."

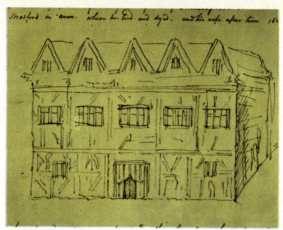

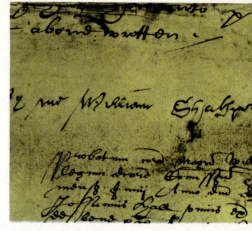

*Right: New Place, the house which the poet bought in 1597 for £60 and where he ended his days. It was one of the grandest residences in Stratford, with its three storeys and five gables. The photograph below shows a tranquil view of the town. On the far right we see Shakespeare's third signature to his will.*

# LAST DAYS IN THE QUIET OF STRATFORD

In his will, having nominated his favourite daughter Susanna and her husband virtually the sole heirs to his fortune, he went on to leave minor bequests to many people. To Judith a small legacy; to the poor of the parish he left £10; to his fellow actors Burbage, Heming and Condell he left 26s. 8d. each, "to buy them Ringes"; to relations, friends and neighbours he left various personal belongings. Rather late he remembered his wife, Anne, in an addition made at the time of the revision: "I gyve unto my wief my second best bed with the furniture" (the word furniture meant hangings). This was very little, but perhaps his wife had expressed the wish to live with her children on her husband's death. Having put his affairs in order, William Shakespeare died. Perhaps he had already been ill when, legend has it, Michael Drayton and Ben Jonson came to visit him. With them he would have drunk a great deal while remembering old times, perhaps enough to send him to his sickbed. This hypothesis, if not verifiable, is a possible one which will perhaps displease those who persist in seeing Shakespeare as a romantic hero, unblemished but also not quite human. Whatever may have been the cause of his death the end came on April 23, 1616, the day of his 52nd birthday. The poet, who believed in the magic of numbers, perhaps remembered the words he gave to Cassius shortly before he died: "This day I breathed first; time is come round, And where I did begin, there shall I end; My life is run his compass". On April 25, Shakespeare was buried in the Church of the Holy Trinity; his death is recorded in the same parish register as his baptism. There is no name on his tombstone, only this epitaph which he is thought to have written himself: "Good friend, for Jesus' sake forbeare To digg the dust enclosed heare! Bleste be the man that spares thes stones And curst be he that moves my bones". Perhaps this invocation is the reason that no man has ever dared to disturb Shakespeare's grave. For 350 years "sweet Shakespeare" has rested in peace within the chancel of his church. Close by, a monument has been erected but his true monument was the publication of his first folio by Heming and Condell, without which it is possible that the world would not have remembered Shakespeare or his works.

# HE NEVER TROUBLED TO HAVE HIS WORKS PUBLISHED

*In a niche in the wall of the church, not far from his tombstone, is a bust of Shakespeare placed there shortly after his death. It was painted to compensate with colour what it undoubtedly lacked in sculptural qualities. As this bust was made during the lifetime of his wife, daughters and friends, we must presume that it bears some resemblance to the poet. The portrait on the opposite page is probably a good likeness, as his friends Heming and Condell included it in the volume of collected works which they published seven years after his death. Shakespeare had never bothered to have his works published, with the exception of his first two poems, and the* Sonnets. *During his lifetime about 15 of his comedies and tragedies had been printed in an unauthorized edition. To repair this and prevent any future damage the two colleagues patiently gathered the texts of 36 works and had them published, "without any personal ambition or desire to profit but only to keep alive the memory of a worthy friend that was our Shakespeare". And so the first folio came into existence, a volume of nearly 900 pages with a dedication by Ben Jonson. About two hundred copies of this edition exist today. It is a bizarre reminder of the status of the professional writer in Shakespeare's time and also perhaps of his own lack of literary vanity that scholars have disputed and will continue to dispute the accuracy of texts which Shakespeare never saw in book form, and did not even revise for publication.*

If it is impossible to describe in a few words Shakespeare's genius, we can try to sum up briefly the information gathered on his work, his period and, from what little has been recorded, the life of the dramatist. His main feature seems to be a very great understanding of man—his life, his pain, his "life sickness". To this we can add his extraordinary ability to express anything poetically and directly. His best-known character, Hamlet, has been studied in every way —from the romantic, the Freudian, the existential angle, and has repaid the needs of every age. His great tragedies, *Macbeth, Othello, King Lear,* speak in a voice which makes irrelevant our lack of biographical knowledge. He was not a great scholar, neither was he a traveller and it would be pointless to seek in his works geographical or historical accuracy. He did not travel the world, but he gave life to a world of which he was the sole creator; a complete world containing its own truth; "The rest is silence". Ben Jonson, his friend and rival, said of Shakespeare some years after his death: "He was not of an age but for all time".

**1564** –April 23: William Shakespeare was born at Stratford-on-Avon, the third of eight children of John Shakespeare, originally a tenant farmer, later a businessman, and of Mary Arden, descendant of an ancient family of land owners. The father was probably a Catholic, in fact his name is listed as a "recusant"—a Catholic who had deserted the Church of England.

**1566** – James VI of Scotland born in Edinburgh; he later became James I of England.

**1570** – Pope Pius V excommunicated Elizabeth of England. The Lord Mayor of London forbade performances by actors within the city walls; the first theatres built in the capital were situated outside the city.

**1572** – August 23-4: Massacre of St. Bartholomew's Day in France.

**1576** – James Burbage built London's first theatre in Shoreditch.

**1577** – Drake's voyage around the world.

**1582** – William Shakespeare married Anne Hathaway, eight years his senior.

**1587** – February 8: Mary Stuart's execution. The year Shakespeare went to London in search of his fortune. In 1592 he was an established actor and writer.

**1588** – End of July: defeat of the "Invincible Armada".

**1591-2** – *A Comedy of Errors,* a farce.

**1592-4** – A certain familiarity with Italian geography which he shows in some of his plays had led some to believe that he visited Italy during this time. He certainly knew John Florio, teacher of Italian in the house of Southampton. Southampton was Shakespeare's patron and it was to him that the poet dedicated *Venus and Adonis* in 1593 and *The Rape of Lucrece* the following year. The former poem was described by Shakespeare as the "first heir of my invention".

**1593** – Christopher Marlowe killed in a tavern brawl.

**1593-4** –Shakespeare wrote *Titus Andronicus* and *The Taming of the Shrew*.

**1594-5** – *Romeo and Juliet,* inspired by a novel by Bandello.

**1595** – *A Midsummer Night's Dream.* The "Swan" Theatre was built in London. The Irish Uprising.

**1595-6** – *Richard II,* dramatic history.

**1596** – Shakespeare's petition to the College of Heralds for a family coat-of-arms. Wrote *The Merchant of Venice*.

**1597-8** – *Henry IV.*

**1598** – *Much Ado about Nothing.*

**1599** – Shakespeare's company opened the "Globe" Theatre. Also the "Fortune" Theatre was built. Essex's expedition to Ireland; later he figures in the tragedy *Henry V.* Also in this year, *As You Like It*.

**1599-1600** – *Twelfth Night* and *Julius Caesar*.

**1600** – Giordano Bruno burned at the stake.

**1600-1** – *The Merry Wives of Windsor,* comedy.

**1601** – February 10: *Richard II*

presented at the "Globe" Theatre. February 8: Essex's plot against Queen Elizabeth discovered. The performance of the day before had been requested by his followers in the hope of making the spectators rise against the Queen. February 25: execution of Essex. In this year Shakespeare put the finishing touches to *Hamlet*.

**1602-3** – *All's Well that Ends Well.*

**1603** – March 24: Elizabeth I of England died after 45 years on the throne. James I, passionately fond of the theatre, ascended the throne. Shakespeare's company became the "King's Men".

**1604-5** – *Othello.*

**1605** – The Gunpowder Plot.

**1605-6** – Shakespeare wrote *King Lear* and *Macbeth*.

**1606** – Birth of Corneille.

**1606-7** – *Antony and Cleopatra.*

**1607-8** – *Coriolanus.*

**1609** – Publication of the *Sonnets,* which Shakespeare had written some years previously.

**1610** – Shakespeare retired to Stratford where in the preceding years he had acquired property, and there he peacefully spent his last years.

**1611** – *The Tempest,* possibly the last work he was to write by himself.

**1613** – June 29: The "Globe" is destroyed by fire caused by gunshots during a performance of *Henry VIII,* which Shakespeare is said to have written in collaboration with others.

**1616** – April 23: death of Shakespeare.